Guiding Grace Series – Volume II

Golden Wisdom of Love Legends & Legacies

To linda & Jerome,
Thank you for being legends
to me whom I love.

Thomas Baldrick

Stories Compiled by

Sandy Rogers and Sharyn G. Jordan

Christmas 2022

©2022 All Rights Reserved.
Golden Wisdom of Love Legends and Legacies
Guiding Grace Series – Volume II
Compiled by Sandy Rogers and Sharyn G. Jordan

Paperback ISBN: 978-1-958405-44-4
Hardcover ISBN: 978-1-958405-45-1
eBook ISBN: 978-1-958405-43-7
Library of Congress Control Number: 2022920255

Publisher: Spotlight Publishing House™
Triangulus 3 Publishing

https://spotlightpublishinghouse.com
Main Editor: Sandy Rogers, Sharyn G. Jordan
Interior Design: Marigold2k
Cover Design: Krunal Patel

www.tri3pub.com

Guiding Grace Series – Volume II

Golden Wisdom of Love Legends & Legacies

Stories Compiled by

Sandy Rogers and Sharyn G. Jordan

Spotlight PUBLISHING House

Goodyear, Arizona

Contents

Dedication

*"Raise your words, not your voice.
It is rain that grows flowers, not thunder."*

-Rumi

Think of our Golden Wisdom of Love, Legends & Legacies compendium as a Garden of Grace.

Our Authors are Stewards of Mercy whose stories seed, cultivate, grow, and bloom words that inspire, edify, move, & heal.

Together, we are planting flowered fields of perennial elegance, exquisite empathy, kindness, compassion, courage, & connectivity.

Preface

TRIANGULUS 3
PUBLISHING

Navigating the Uncharted Seas of Your Sacred Story

The word preface comes from the Latin "prae" and "fotia," meaning spoken before. In a book, its goal is to provide the reader with its history, why, how the project came into being and the inspiration behind its story. In our Guiding Grace, Wisdom of the Silver Sisters book, we shared how this noble enterprise magically unfolded. We took the Readerly down our unexpected rabbit holes, the confidences that bridged what could have been major gaps, and along the way, we shared the valuable skillsets learned. Having now grown into our publishing potential, here we are once again. We are ecstatic to find ourselves in the center of this writerly universe in the divine company of fellow sojourners who answered the call of their Writerly Souls. As we know, synchronicity is always for us.

To sing our authors' praises, in early 2021, we founded Triangulus 3 Publishing, LLC. The name and original logo are a generous gift from my co-compiler, Sandy Rogers' consulting company, whose artwork was first inspired by a stunning piece of Celtic jewelry she was wearing. It was an eternal knot charm woven into a triangle. More synchronicity? Methinks so! The triangle itself is a fire symbol whose shape denotes joy, clarity, enthusiasm, enlightenment, illumination, and luminosity and holds the energy of a mythological Sun God, the Phoenix. This is especially apropos as many of our writers have risen from the ashes of trauma, heartbreak, and/or a serious illness. The power of REbirth, REsurrection, and REfinement inspired these innovative authors to eliminate anything superfluous and all things REdundant.

Initially, our Triangulus 3 Publishing's logo artist was REndered by a row of three triangles standing in front of the other. Front to back, we selected the colors of sage green for our books' evergreen and sagacious intentions. The second triangle is the color Silver, an homage to our first anthology project, plus it symbolizes the muse. Since Sandy and I both relish the color purple, our third hue was a given. We were especially pleased with our choices. In REtrospect, they served our authors well.

The first part of 2022, Sandy was inspired to reach out to our artist to create a 5D version of our logo. He presented the emblematic artwork we now enjoy within a very short time. Looking upon it, we saw its symbolic REsemblance to a sailboat…indeed, sail on silver girls. I love that Paul Simon wrote his famous lyrics as a nod to his then wife upon seeing her first grey hair. It was also indicative of our mission to serve our authors with the vast oceanic abundance and exquisitely express themselves. Thinking of this life as a voyage, the metaphoric imagery of writing, as in sailing the open seas of our soul, confidently takes us beyond the safety of harbored shores. So, let us raise the mast of our mighty pen, set sail on the blank page, and confidently navigate the uncertain seas of our sacred story. Every written word brings us deeper into the REcesses of our Being; the discovery of who we are.

Our heartfelt intention remains steadfast from all its incarnations including the Celtic knot, triple triangles and now the stylized sailboat. We invite you to adventure into our eclectic and magical journey of the heart. Quoting the Wisdom of the Silver Sister's Preface, "Our brave authors' experiential stories have shown up as the joys of whimsy, the admirable disciple of unfolding professional profoundness… sharing the power of legacy, the despair of brokenness that led to healing and even time travel. Each chapter is compelling and inspirational, and although you will resonate with most, the stories are foreign to your life so far. BE Bold, BE a World-Builder, and above all, BE A Storyteller!

We are BEyond Grateful to announce our *Guiding Grace Series, Volume II*'s newest feature titled *The Homage.* We are showcasing authors whose books represent the power of story. You, too, will BE Inspired by their sacred journey. The discipline REquired to write a book, much less publish it, is enormous. Just as our Anthology's Contributing Authors, we instinctively sought out the openings to write and learned to look past all the potential obstacles, switchbacks, setbacks, and possible excuses for never having penned even one word to paper. Instead, we championed the challenges, and now, you have in your hands an Oracle of sorts, a luminous light showing you the Writerly Way of *Golden Wisdom, Love, Legends, and Legacies.* My darling, you too can conquer your greatest fears… therefore, write onward!

Deep Bow,
Sharyn G. Jordan
Storyteller

Prologue

*"Go confidently in the direction of your dreams.
Live the life you have imagined."*

~Henry David Thoreau

The purpose of a Prologue is to introduce the book's scope of literary work, establish its backstory and set the mood. With our glowing **Golden Wisdom of Love, Legends, & Legacies** title, as you can imagine, our stories range from being emotionally heartfelt to breaking every rule in the How-to-Succeed in Business by listening to the whispers of the soul and achieving lofty goals. Inspirational experiences that take and break us to the brink of life's edges where the author was able to polish the jagged fringes just enough to not only survive, but to thrive.

After a medical diagnosis of imminent death, one author's blog went far beyond writing as it connected her with a greater reason to live and she continues to defy the odds. Far and wide; high and low, the power of story challenges us to be more inclusive as in moving humanity forward. To BE Imaginists, who create workable solutions to global issues, being better aligned with meaningful purposes, and mastering an ancient craft called The Tao of Living Exquisitely. Indeed, *Love, Legends, & Legacies* are essential parts of our magic, miracles, and inner muse. Thank you for being here.

Guiding Grace Series, Volume II brings our authentic authors' stellar stories of how to trust, lean into and embrace the delays, detours, and disappointments into real life. How learning to celebrate the joys hidden beneath sorrow, the gladness on the other side of grief, and the lasting blessings once obscured by fear is essential. These worthy values comprise the steadfast triumphs of *Love, Legends, & Legacies.* Our stories attest to the brilliance of vision, believing in our mighty missions, and fusing functionality with beauty. To honor their unique voice, each chapter, has remained in its originally submitted format, and yes, we set our own mood as in attitude. Writing from our HeART, we wrapped our intentional words into exceptional narratives dispelling all myths, magnificently broadening our fields of awareness, and sharpening our focus. As we know, *"Where Attention Goes, Elegantly, Energy Flows."*

Indeed, as Thoreau encouraged, we are living the life we imagined. Our chapters illustrate the audacity of personally, professionally, and creatively fulfilling inspired intentions. Each story unfolds the process of discovery; perhaps it was as mentioned above, an illness, the loss of a loved one, or a childhood suffering that brought about the realization of transformation's active force during challenges. The healing mercy of surrender and/or the grace of a magnificent mentorship. These once difficult experiences became blessings and redirected our path into positive change. As we know, we are the stories we tell ourselves.

Although our stories will differ extensively, yet at the core, it is our collective journey of courage that beautifully improves the quality of everyone's life. Our contributions address dwelling in harmony, deepening inner strength as now we positively influence cherished social values. Our expansive endeavor answered destiny aka humanity's call for empathy, to evolve the status quo, and the necessity to edify one another. Boldy, we faced the tests, illusions, and lessons of our odyssey. You will commiserate with our journeys of the soul; and yes, will BE Inspired. As road weary sojourners, often exhausted, yet we never gave up hope. If we did, it was only for a minute. Wandering far and wide, following the luminous beacon of *Love, Legends, & Legacies*; and we found our way home.

Love

> *"Love is a valuable, high-frequency emotion that defines, refines, and, and reveals our greater sense of purpose. Dwelling in it is profoundly joyful."*

~Sharyn G. Jordan

In a world trying to redefine itself, our emotionally integrous *Love* stories are deeply impactful. Truly, *Love* is the ultimate in energetic value. Per 1 Corinthians, 13:13, "Now three things will last forever ~ faith, hope, and love ~ and the greatest of these is *love.*" Indeed, you will BE inspired by the depth of our fellow sojourners' commitments. Our divine story takes us into the meaningfulness of how a spouse, sibling, or even a son's influence helped us to better understand life's circuitous path. It significantly enhanced our presence, and worthiness, and was sublimely metamorphic. Being. gifting the Writerly such substantial progress, we were blessed with major breakthroughs. In addition, experience the unveiling of lasting self-love. To live a life of creative fulfillment, this process is essential.

Possibly, our story celebrates a cherished friendship whose enthusiasm was so infectious it elevated our sense of worth. In turn, we learned to trust our chosen path and became a mentor, a way-shower for others.

Through a rocky road full of unexpected twists and surprising turns of events, perhaps our author scribed an homage of gratitude for their loved one(s). The people who through thick and thin, faithfully stayed by the author's side. As Geo. Eliot noted, "Blessed is the influence of one true, loving soul on another." Once we experience this divine State of BEing, we can live in the radiant realm of clarity, compassion, connection; and yes, courage. Trailblazing became one of our superpowers.

Legends

> *"A hero is someone who has given his or her life*
> *to something bigger than oneself."*

-Joseph Campbell

A *Legend* is someone who creates an unforgettable impression, impacts the world on a incredible level and is an ordinary person doing extraordinary things. The first step when honoring a potential *Legend* is to recognize their innate talent. In the Shero/Hero Journey, Joseph Campbell teaches us that by answering destiny's adventurous call, and 'Following our Bliss, the Universe will open doors for you where there were only walls." A *Legend* has a deeper sense of self-awareness and unveils the profoundly rewarding secrets to honestly assess, access, and pursue the greater purposes of life.

These larger-than-life *Legends* paved the way for the author to escape a toxic environment, outgrow limiting world views, and overcome their deepest fears. As *Legends*, they continue to cultivate a beautiful, satisfying lifestyle. They are emotionally available, an advocate for the greater good of the greatest number of people and are grounded. *Legends* understand the responsibility of leadership and use whatever opportunities they've been granted to prosper. A *Legend* enjoys an inner and outer abundance wafting all 'round and naturally understands life's opulent openings to BE the Difference and step into the role.

Legacies

"The Universe is transformation.
Life is what our thoughts make it."

~Marcus Aurelius

A **Legacy** may include an endowment of funds, philanthropic endeavors, an impressive bank balance, vast properties, gems, jewels, gold, and silver. Indeed, true wealth is not only found in our values, our families, and perhaps the causes that we build and continue to live on, without our supervision. It is also our spiritual impact on those around us and those who come after us. **Legacy** absolutely focuses on the intangibles that a person creates such as kindness, generosity, and social responsibility. It consists of their ethics, their contributions in making the world a better place, and a positive example of being an enthusiastic advocate. By asking ourselves, what have we created that will live long, and survive after I am gone, the answer uncovers the benefits of our legacies.

When **Legacy** is bequeathed, there is an opportunity for hearts to be opened, veils lifted, and to evoke the highest nature of humanity. This part nurtures others' genius and inspires them to develop their creativity to BE Energetic World Builders who enthusiastically expand consciousness and cultivate compassion. Perhaps you'll expand your ideas of who you are as an artist, writer, mom or dad, grandparent, equestrian, and of course, a more caring human that leaves a Legacy just by Being Yourself. I do know our stories will deepen, shape, and develop your sensibilities, enable you to recognize the magical synchronicities unfolding just for you, and discover the sweet sacredness found in the commonplace, For you, may the divine blessings set forth within the profound pages of our *Golden Wisdom of Love, and Legends & Legacies* BE Perpetual.

Scan the QR code with your smartphone or go to:
https://youtu.be/bVjj2XIurvk

Foreword

By Thomas Baldrick

A heartfelt congratulations on finding this unique book. May you realize it is no coincidence or accident. Pay attention for the messages clearly meant for you.

Perhaps there is even something in this foreword that provides you a feeling of hope, a good laugh, or even something uncomfortable but good. How about an unfulfilled longing of yours rising to the surface (yet again) ...while there is still time for you to act on it?

Yes. You can reinvent yourself and transform any legend and legacy. I'm living proof.

My name is Thomas Baldrick. I've been blessed in my career as a television reporter and producer. I've spent time with U.S. Presidents, movie stars, music stars, TV stars, and take-charge military and corporate leaders. I've spent time with world-class athletes and some world-class a-holes, too.

- I've been on the receiving end of a Donald Trump meltdown, which came in endless waves. (My not backing down or being able to hold in laughing didn't help). And I've received my share of affectionately delivered F-bombs from Joe Biden.

- I still regret jumping on the back of a great cameraman to prevent him from beating the crap out of actor Chris Tucker. I wanted the job myself. Yet, I do wear of badge of honor for telling a rude Don Shula, "Remember Pal, you're just a football coach." (He made the story even better by becoming the winningest coach in NFL history).

- I've been punched in the nose by an angry Dick Clark. And I've punched Mike Tyson in the stomach as hard as I could, only to have him punch back by giggling.

- I've been bounced for asking Britney Spears too hard of a question. And I've had a home run baseball hit by Lance Parrish bounce off my hard head while interviewing Hall of Famer Mike Schmidt.

- I've been mesmerized by the sweetness and beauty of Alicia Keys and Bo Derek. And I nearly suffocated from laughing with Billy Crystal.

- I've taken excited little girls to meet Justin Timberlake. And got a shirtless Phil Collins to play the bagpipes on camera. I've ridden in a limo with Howard Stern and on an airplane with a murderer just acquitted on all charges.

- I was voted by my peers to be the only reporter on the scene for the amazing "Miracle of the Miners" rescue. And I'm still not overworking in New York City on September 11, 2001. Since then, when people ask me how I'm doing, I say, "I'm great. I woke up today." They always laugh. While I'm always serious about my gratitude.

- In closing, the great Diane Sawyer used to call me "The Legend." And my "Six degrees of Kevin Bacon" includes interviewing both him and his Dad.

What is the point of telling you all this? A big part of it is to get your attention. Plus, I was asked to write this foreword because of having stories to tell.

That high-profile information and much more like it is what I often call "My smoke and mirrors." To many people, it could be the stuff of what legends and legacies are made of. And that is fine. Don't get me wrong. I freely admit these stories make for great material in speeches and over cocktails, too.

But for me, and any potential legend or legacy I create or leave behind, I prefer looking elsewhere. I like to go within. For some reason, I must. Maybe it's because I feel like I have lived multiple incarnations inside this same body.

Decades later, the 4-year-old who had his "Pop Pop" and hero fall into his little lap and die still remembers every moment like it was yesterday. Same for the boy who still manages the toxic residue of the cruel "unthinkables" from his mother.

The epic "wild child" and "party animal" young man who committed every act of stupidity, either pre-meditated or spontaneously, have either matured or gotten bored or tired. The likely answer is tired.

And what about the true Pisces (the most sensitive men on the planet)? The guy who emerged in his late 20s remains deeply spiritual, highly intuitive, and kinesthetic. He who often feels misunderstood and underestimated and a bit too far out there for most folks. That dude is alive and well but still studying, learning, going, and growing on this extraordinary journey.

Life seems to have given me an awful lot for one legacy. So, I create new ones, like new chapters. And should you be open to this practice, you can do it, too.

I think about a life legacy because I think about dying, and it is not because I am afraid or in poor health. You see, I am also someone who has experienced speeding through the afterlife's multi-colored tunnel toward the blinding white light. Absolutely, positively, I wanted to stay "on the other side." I was literally bawling my eyes out when told I had to go back.

My only child, Julian Baldrick, is the main reason I think about dying. Selfishly, I don't ever want to leave him. Though as a solo parent for most of his 16 years, I am doing better than I thought in letting him go to live his life. Legend or legacy come what may.

Julian's birth in 2005 changed my life and my legacy in ways that cannot be explained or undone. I'm good with that. I'm good with the choices and sacrifices I have made to be the Daddy we both wanted and needed me to be. Yet, I carry shame for being steamrolled by the marriage which brought him to life—putting the steamroller in reverse over my self-image only created further damage.

Which leads to the new legacy I created after making a comeback even stronger than my worst setback. It is the one allowing me to feel proud and grateful for who I am.

Never once have I spanked or verbally shamed my son. By need as much as choice, I have been a loving but relentless father and teacher who leads by example. The pillars of our 2-person home are fun, trust, honesty, respect, keeping your word, owning mistakes and apologizing, thinking positive, and always and all ways saying, "I love you."

Eventually, we all come to a fork in the road (especially as a parent). If we choose to repeat the hurts and wrongs of our childhood development, we go left. If we want to replace them with love and wisdom, we go right; we do right.

For what it's worth, if your legend and legacy are important to you, it is up to you to establish, nurture, and grow them. If you want your world to know about it, then self-promotion is not only a good thing but also a wise choice. Read that a second time if you must.

Here is what I mean. The speed of daily life seems to be growing faster than the murder rate, the melting of glaciers, and the drying up of water combined. With the non-stop distraction of technology, the rush to judgment, and the immeasurable lightning-quick changes to the world taking place, I consciously and actively reinforce my legacy with whom and where it matters most to me. In my case, I remind my son and will also remind my wife should I be lucky to find her one day.

Here are some recent examples:

- Driving 425 miles between Arizona and Mexico just to apologize *in person* to a family whose reservation of our rental condo got accidentally botched. I told my son, "This is how I hope you will remember me when I'm gone."

- Taking three days to transport the coolest one-eyed German Shepherd puppy rescued from dog fighting in Mexico to hit the jackpot with his loving adopted forever family north of Seattle. I told my son, "This is how I hope you will remember me when I'm gone."

- Being different than all the gawkers outside the supermarket where my son got his first job. Instead of looking with disgust at a drunk, transient man out cold in the brutal Arizona heat, I was the one showing him kindness. Asking to talk to him, sitting him up against a wall, getting him water and food, and calling for the awesome paramedics who got the man medical attention. After my son saw his ride home from work was the guy who did this, I said, "I know you're a teenager, but I hope I didn't embarrass you because this is what I teach you and how I hope you will remember me when I'm gone." Julian replied, "No, Dad, I'm proud of you. That was awesome."

This alone shows you by living your life as the person you want to be, you can create and leave the legend and legacy you wish to have. Now to this book specifically.

I've met Sharyn Jordan. She seems like a lovely woman. And being partners with Sandy Rogers would fill in any gaps for me. You see, Sandy is my dear friend. She is a beautiful, kind, and courageous woman with a sacred human heart. So, I'm honored to play a small role in this latest publication of the growing legacy of this dynamic duo.

So go ahead. Judge this book by its cover. It's the least we can do in showing support for "Golden Wisdom of Love Legends & Legacies.

"Leap first, and the rope shall appear." I love this saying and have loved living it countless times. It describes what Sandy Rogers and Sharyn Jordan have done in committing to acting on their latest idea for a book. Then, 35 more individuals from all walks of life answered the call by taking a similar leap of faith in sharing their stories.

My hope is life changes for all of those behind this book and all of those who are compelled to read it.

In closing, if you are like many, you may equate your self-value by how much wealth you have accumulated, what your job title is, how religious you are, the followers you have for your selfies, the homes you own, or the cars you drive. And that's all fine, too. But even if it is just for a moment of exploration, I invite you to go within. It's never too late to be who you really crave to be deep down inside.

Maybe just maybe, the widespread hatred, violence, depression, and addictions could be lessened if more people focused on being the best version of themselves in creating their own legend or legacy.

Thank you for your time. I am honored to be among kindred spirits.

Namaste,
Thomas Baldrick

Thomas Baldrick

Wounded child.

Grew to be a protector.

Devoted longtime Solo Dad of Julian Baldrick.

Creative Thinker, Writer, Host Producer.

7-Time Emmy Award Winner.

Gave 2 statues to children.

Another in a Vision Quest Giveaway Ceremony.

Curious and always learning. Fun, but doesn't laugh enough.

Unusually Kind by Choice.

Born with Philly DNA. Resides in Arizona desert. Doesn't like drinking water.

Never met a stranger but always helps them. Works out daily to consume pizza, beer, margaritas, candy. Enjoys silence but talks to everyone. Single. Sensitive Pisces. Keeps his word. Holder of Hope and Dreams.

(480) 415-8610
www.Baldrick.com

Dreams of the Soul

The Artist

The Fisherman

By Alicia Bravo

"The people who get on in this world are the people who get up and look for the circumstances they want, and if they can't find them, make them."

~ George Bernard Shaw (1856 – 1950)

Dreams of the Soul

The Artist
The Fisherman

By Alicia Bravo

The Artist

We all have dreams. Many of our dreams tend to be focused on what we want as individuals. But a dream that serves a higher purpose at a soul level that will ultimately serve all of humanity and beyond is a legacy that is a true gift.

I was casually walking along the stores in the Fairfax district in Los Angeles when I ran across an art gallery that struck an interest from the paintings I viewed in the window. There I saw unique wall after wall of paintings of faces clustered one by one, as if in a gathering in the painting. Many very intriguing faces were gazing back at me in multiples. I saw the attention-grabbing expressions that each face had in the painting with multiple personalities on each face, all unique and different.

Then I ran across a painting that indicated this was no ordinary artist. He had a true gift of seeing souls, and people at a deeper level. This painting was so unusual and illustrated a birthing of souls coming up from the ocean water at the North Pole.

The souls were surfacing through a tunnel through a glacier, and they were all such happy faces as they were being birthed coming to life in the painting. It struck me that this artist could see the lost souls of these human beings and was giving them an uninterrupted bridge of being seen by others because of his paintings.

Other paintings were quite different, but they also showed lost souls in various scenarios of being seen by others, perhaps for the first time.

Some of the souls were animals, primarily dogs. I had never seen any paintings like these before. They were magnificent!

I asked the artist what his inspiration was for his paintings. He said it came to him in his dreams and that he could see the faces. So, he had to paint from inspiration. I could see that they were lost souls who were now being seen for the first time through his paintings.

The artist shared that since he was now an old man, he dreamed that his paintings, these specific ones, would be placed in the Los Angeles Museum of Art and he would donate them so others could see these specific paintings. These paintings were not for sale like his other paintings but were solely for those to enjoy his wonderful art and legacy. He dreamt that before his death, the Museum would accept his donation to be displayed for all to see. The artist had lived a full life of his vision for people to see those lost souls who had never been seen.

The Fisherman

Twenty years ago, I purchased land in Mexico on the beach in Puerto Peñasco. I had been going there for years and wanted a beach home later for retirement and respite. This beach was way out of town and quite peaceful, and not many houses or anything else was out there. The night sky and the beautiful turquoise Sea of Cortez always gave me a sense of peace and tranquility.

Now twenty years later, I wanted to investigate putting a home on the parcel in this quiet beach area. The landowner and I met and talked it over at his office. He wanted to show me the project for his entire parcels of land, which was vast and stretched for miles far and wide, beyond where my beach home would be. He had this dream of developing a vast project that would include a marina and grocery stores, hotels, gas stations, 10,000 houses, and a sustainable desalinization water plant for drinkable and potable water.

He was very passionate about putting a desalinization plant to provide water for the community and jobs for people. He said it was his dream to have this project come to fruition. He talked about it every time I went to meet with him about my home project. His face would just light up with excitement every time he talked about it. Then he said he was approached by a company in San Diego that was going to buy his land and develop it. The San Diego developer was going to put a desalinization plant there to run a line of water from his beach land all the way to supply water for Phoenix and Tucson, Arizona, as well as Las Vegas, Nevada. His dream was to see this happen before he dies.

He had been a simple fisherman all his life and purchased this land back in the 1960s. Everyone thought he was crazy for purchasing this land so far out and so much of it. It's miles and miles of gorgeous beach and sand. He worked hard all his life to provide for his family as a fisherman. Now he's older and facing health problems. His dream is to see this project come true. A legacy that feeds others water, provides jobs and serves another country as well as his own. He knows the Sea of Cortez very well. As a retired fisherman who always welcomes me and my family with fantastic local caught fish and shrimp dinners, I truly hope his dream comes true.

I also have a dream, a personal one to have a beach house in Mexico on that beach. My dream is so small, and I realized that my self-serving dream had to become more than just this. I want to dream bigger, dream about how I can serve a higher purpose for humanity like the artist and the fisherman, who have the desire to see their dreams come true before they die. They want to live and ask God for one more day, one more chance to live to see their dreams come to pass before they do. Even if they pass before their dreams come true, they have already provided a legacy for humanity.

They have both inspired me to dream bigger and how I can write to seek out more people like these great men who are passing down a legacy of their own big dreams to share with others. I hope that these stories have inspired you to dream bigger as well. Manifestation is made real by dreaming and dreaming big.

Alicia Bravo

Alicia Bravo grew up in Phoenix, Arizona. She's a very passionate intuitive writer, and a hair salon owner. Since the beginning of her career, her first love was writing. This led to life experiences such as confessions and juicy secrets heard from behind her stylist's chair.

Alicia is of Spanish and French descent, growing up speaking fluent Spanish with her hermanos and hermanas. Alicia takes the time to get to know people, which opens up insights about each person. Being able to see people for who they truly are and listening closely to their stories represent her greatest gifts.

CONTACT INFORMATION:

480-951-8076
Oz.aj.wizard@me.com
https://instagram.com/bravosalonaz
https://facebook.com/bravosalonaz
https://bravosalonaz.com
https://www.linkedin.com/in/alicia-bravo-18942511

The Table

By Andrea Brundage

There's a seat at my table
It's open to you
The lonely, forgotten
the heartbroken, too.

the joyful, the mourning
the whole and the wounded
imperfectly
perfect
and wonderfully human

Should you be wayfaring
and knock at my door
there's a seat at
my table
You'll know who it's for.

A Seat at My Table

~ Gwen Buckles

Chapter 2

The Table

By Andrea Brundage

It was a nice house on a rectangularly-shaped lot in a small town in Southern California. My dad built it in 1960, and I lived there with my mom, dad, an older sister, and three older brothers.

Mom referred to the house next door as *The Little House*. They all lived there before I came along. From mom's perspective, dad was taking too long to finish the new house, and she was about to deliver a baby – me! She was eager to move in and get settled, so she moved the family in before the house was completed. Side note: Dad had a habit of taking his time. Mom had a habit of getting shit done.

Edgar Avenue was lined with blooming olive trees (achoo!), eucalyptus trees, some stately lilacs, and a few large pines. Some yards were painted rock – that's where the old people lived – while others had well-manicured lawns. The cemetery at the end of the block was a grassy playground for neighborhood kids.

Our backyard had several fruit trees, some pretty rose bushes, and a huge walnut tree. The sturdy branches of the walnut tree made the perfect ladder for accessing the garage roof. While I despised the chore of husking those dirty walnuts, I loved spending time in that tree, and on that roof.

There was a dirt basketball court out back, and the neighborhood kids would show up to play. I loved watching my brothers and their friends play sports, and even though I was much younger, they let me join in on occasion.

There's an 8mm film of me at about age 3 playing football with my brothers and the neighbor kids. The yellow and blue Los Angeles Rams helmet on my head was huge, but I was ready! Hut-hut, I was handed the football, and off I went. The older boys fell out of the way, and I raced towards the imaginary goal line. Touchdown! Surely, this was the beginning of my love of sports, and team, and oh, winning! Maybe this was also when I learned that I could accomplish whatever I set my mind to.

Our gathering place inside the house was the kitchen table. It's where mom and dad drank morning coffee before heading off to work, and where I, in my sleepy-eyed stupor, would often join them. I vividly remember waking to the aroma of percolating coffee and feeling joyful. All these years later, I still love that smell.

The table was where we played cards and games. It's where my sister and I played Concentration, and where my brother taught me Cribbage. Other games included Gin Rummy, Yahtzee, Nibs, Spoons, Skip-Bo, and Scrabble. Once I watched while they messed around with a Ouija board. Mom had been to the green stamps store, and she came back with it. I wasn't allowed to play and, very unlike me, I didn't want to play anyway. Even as a kid, it felt creepy to me.

We ate meals at the table. As the youngest and the smallest, I was relegated to the back corner against the wall. I rather enjoyed it. My chair was next to the shiny, chrome-plated Sunbeam toaster. During meals, I would make faces and entertain myself. This habit of watching myself didn't go unnoticed by my siblings. With the popularity of the sitcom *My Mother the Car*, I was often referred to as *My Sister the Toaster*.

All business was conducted at the table. I remember the Jewel Tea man, the Fuller Brush man, the Collier's Encyclopedia man, and the Kirby vacuum salesman.

Mom had a manual typewriter that did fancy cursive. Once in a while she'd pull it out of its brown leather case and place it on the table to use. I loved pecking those keys to write letters, usually to my grandmother and cousins who lived far away.

Hours of homework were facilitated at the table. Often present was an encyclopedia or two, plus our huge dictionary. Permission slips, report cards, Scholastic Book order forms – all were left on the table.

It was a particularly great day when the Sears Roebuck Christmas catalog arrived. My brother and I would sit at the table and fold down the page corners to notate the treasures we wanted. Surely, this was helpful to Santa.

There were occasional visits from out-of-town family members. My paternal grandmother, affectionately called Naner, lived in Texas and would visit once or twice a year. She was an avid card player and had a unique way of shuffling. Instead of holding the cards the long way (horizontally), she held them by the short sides (vertically). Her routine was fascinating! She'd shuffle (riffle) once followed by a FAST overhand shuffle. *Riffle, shuffle, repeat.* When I was four, I accompanied Naner on a Greyhound bus trek from California to Tacoma, Washington. We went to visit my aunt, who was her daughter. I don't remember the bus ride, but I distinctly remember that I learned to shuffle on that trip! I came back quite proud to demonstrate my shuffling prowess to my family. And I was particularly happy to surprise them with a perfectly executed bridge!

When aunts and cousins visited, we kids would run off to play. Mom would brew a pot of coffee and the ladies would talk and laugh for hours. On occasion there would be some crafting — resin grape clusters come to mind.

My sister and brothers got married and started families. When they'd bring their babies over to visit, we'd set the infant carriers in the middle of the table, and we'd commence with the *oohs* and *ahhs* and fits of laughter.

As I revisit memories of growing up and of wonderful times at the table, I am aware it sounds idyllic. It wasn't. Our family had struggles. Dad drank a lot. Mom was the nervous type. One of my brothers was born with severe medical challenges. The table was where mom sat to make phone calls to Los Angeles Children's Hospital to set up appointments for him. It's where she'd spread out paperwork, bills, and taxes, and it's there where she sat trying to figure out how to make ends meet.

Mom took copious notes and wrote letters at the table. I'm sure it's where she decided she couldn't live with my dad anymore. His drinking had progressed into full-blown alcoholism and after 24 years of marriage, she filed for divorce. It was time.

Mom passed away in December 2020. When approached about this project, I thought I'd write a story entitled *Tales of the Tools*. It would be about the joy I get from using a few of my mom's kitchen bowls and utensils. I planned to tell you about the *Pancake Bowl* and how I will only make the batter in *that* green Pyrex bowl. I was going to share how I only use her copper patinaed spatula to remove freshly baked cookies from a cookie sheet. I was going to tell you that the teddy bear toothpick holder reminds me of her every single day. It wasn't meant to be. Not this time.

Dinner's ready. It's time to eat…

…at the table.

Andrea Brundage

Andrea Brundage is a Professional Organizer & Bringer of Calm. Andrea says, "Helping clients create supportive spaces is my gift and my passion." She's been organizing homes and offices for 15+ years. As an expert organizer, published author, speaker, and workshop facilitator, she is a woman on the go. Andrea says, "Turning chaos into calm is my superpower."

Andrea has authored two books: *SIMPLIFY: 8 Simple Principles to Turn Your Chaos into Calm* and *The Organized Estate: A planning booklet.* She also collaborated with 44 other authors on the highly acclaimed book, *Wisdom of the Silver Sisters: Guiding Grace.*

www.AndreaBrundage.com
www.ProfessionalOrganizerAZ.com
(480) 382-1085

Scan the QR code with your smartphone or go to:
https://youtu.be/f_ABtxE_9Bo

Every Silver Lining has a Cloud

By Barbara Palmer

"She stood in the storm, and when the wind did not blow her away, she adjusted her sails."

~ Elizabeth Edwards

Chapter 3

Every Silver Lining Has A Cloud

By Barbara Palmer

Thirty years ago, my husband David and I walked through a door that would literally change our lives. We were so nervous on that moonless night driving toward Arizona State Hospital. (In my growing-up years riding past that intersection of 24th Street and Van Buren, I would peer through the fence to see what a "crazy person" might look like.) Now WE needed help. David and I walked through a door marked NAMI Support Group. NAMI stands for National Alliance for Mental Illness.*

From the dark into the light, we were warmly welcomed by a volunteer who made us feel at home. We joined a circle of strangers who would soon reveal their reason for being there. It would be the first time I would say out loud, "Two of our three sons, Michael and Andy, have been diagnosed with a serious mental illness."

As young parents living under a silver lining, we felt a dark cloud had moved over our family. Our sons were thirteen months apart in age. They were in high school yet attending different schools.

At the age of 16, Andy was hearing voices. He would hear commands coming from the classroom air vents telling him what to do and what not to do. He was horrified enough to ask us for help. Andy would eventually be diagnosed with schizophrenia.*

At the age of 17, Michael walked on his campus feeling like his classmates could see through his clothing. Michael was experiencing delusions and would be diagnosed in time with schizoaffective disorder.*

Our family was a mess! We felt like we were dodging bullets every day with the onslaught of new information.

Our first evening at this support group unveiled familiar yet different mental health-related issues. Isolation, depression, impaired cognitive thinking, and suicidal thinking would rob loved ones of the lives they had known. Mental illness is a brain disorder. Brain disorders affect behavior.

On top of this, another challenge faced us all, stigma, which we would have to shed ourselves. No longer would I EVER refer to patients at Arizona State Hospital or anywhere as "crazy." Instead, I raise my palm high and bless anyone who is obviously suffering the effects of illness. Empathy comes with awareness.

I expected this support group experience to be sober and tearful. Instead, we laughed and listened intently to families courageously pour out their hearts in relief, knowing others recognized themselves in this shared experience. Conversations took place in sworn confidentiality that we weren't ready to have with family and friends. "We called the police last night for help" was heard with empathy and without judgment.

We learned from families a step ahead of us in experience. For instance, we would no longer demand our son's presence at a family holiday event. They would decide for themselves if they could tolerate a large gathering each year.

The learning curve seemed unending, but the information was there for us to find! Did you know that an untreated mental health crisis requires a toolbox of skills?

- Communication skills
- Crisis management skills
- Understanding what our loved one is experiencing
- Learning new vocabulary to put words to our experience
- Knowing who to call for help

Soon, David and I discovered our experience paled in comparison to what Michael and Andy were going through. Still, there is no measure for the heavy toll that is also felt by the whole family. Such deep comfort came from that support group. We went home that first night, shedding shame and feeling hopeful. We slept easier knowing that, with treatment, recovery was possible and even probable.

In the 1980s, science advanced and brought relief to many, including our sons. Michael and Andy would regain some ground and peace of mind, even though their experiences were like night and day from one another.

We are forever grateful to those professionals who helped our sons along the way. Psychologists drew out the boys' stories. Their secret thoughts and struggles were revealed, which they weren't ready to share with their parents. Team building led to a doctor, caseworker, counselor, and support group.

Exhausted as we were, our job as parents became clear. Never let go. And when it seems you need a break, go to a support group or treat yourself to a walk or eat ice cream! We learned to take one step at a time, and our family slowly but surely began to see the light of day.

If our story seems overwhelming, we understand. If you are feeling the weight of our sons' diagnoses, we can only thank you for helping us bare the weight.

Fast forward 24 years. Michael was 40 and Andy 39. David and I rushed through another door. NAMI's Family-to-Family Class had one more opening, and we needed help, fast! Michael was suicidal!

He was over this and just wanted to be "normal." You see, Michael's symptoms included anosognosia.* His failure to not recognize that he was ill and could benefit from medicine didn't stem from denial or being stubborn. Rather, his poor insight into having an illness and the benefits of treatment was ANOTHER SYMPTOM OF THE DISORDER ITSELF.

I was so struck by this concept that my NAMI teaching partner and I attended a weekend training session in San Francisco. Dr. Xavier Amador explained his Columbia University research on anosognosia. He is the author of "*I Am Not Sick I Don't Need Help.*" Fifty percent of seriously ill mental patients experience this condition. That is a shocking statistic.

With community and a wealth of information, NAMI classes helped buffer the blow. I'm sorry to say that Michael died of mental illness by way of suicide on September 23, 2015. Our son became part of a harrowing statistic. We miss our beautiful, gifted musician Michael every day.

What does RECOVERY look like? Andy would tell you that it's having consistent treatment, a daily routine including exercise, secure housing, and purposeful daily activities, which are all essential. He loves caring for the lives of his tree frogs, bonsais, and, believe it or not, a single fish who floats sideways, managing to survive despite all the odds. We gasp when we see this beautiful Betta fish floating on its side, just sure he's a goner. Andy calmly says, "Oh, he's fine."

Treatment doesn't always require medication, but regular counseling seems critical to well-being. Eight years ago, Andy lined up a counselor who not only saw him through his brother's death but serves him well once a month. Andy is an artist in life, and with his jewelry and is working in collaboration with his aunt. He still experiences symptoms but describes the voices are turned down, like the volume on a radio. He inspires people who know him, especially his brother David, his father, and me.

I'll close by saying there is help! Reach out! Walking through one door changed our lives. You are not alone! Mental health is part of every human condition and sometimes needs medical assistance. Recovery comes to most who receive treatment and support. Never give up hope. The storm passes. Today, clear skies.

Barbara Palmer

Barbara is a native Arizonan. Born August 12, 1947, she feels blessed growing up during a time when extended family all lived within close proximity. She is one of five girls, one of them her identical twin. This strong family culture full of togetherness and tradition helped prepare her for what was to come.

Barbara is a mother turned advocate. Loved by her partner of 53 years, David, she raised three sons. Her intention is to encourage and educate families to learn how to live with mental health issues. As a volunteer for NAMI, she is now a voice of *hope*.

NAMI (National Alliance on Mental Illness)
www.nami.org

Scan the QR code with your
smartphone or go to:
https://youtu.be/fRr2tkZ1GHQ

His Legacy is Love

By Betsy Brill

Ntafendaka ntando la mpos'e'ola!

"One does not cross a river by merely longing for home."

~ Congolese proverb

Chapter 4

His Legacy is Love

By Betsy Brill

The 67-year-old man was tall and erect, his silver hair swept away from his handsome face. He was wearing casual business attire that day in 1998. After a stint as an Air Force pilot, the transplanted Midwesterner had begun buying property in Phoenix before it had grown into today's metropolis. He did it all – buying properties, renting, managing, and selling them; bookkeeping and other tasks – even as his wealth grew along with Phoenix. He became a model of success.

As he was led into the Maricopa County jail in 1998, though, he was no longer a mega-successful real estate investor. He and his fellow investors – many of them friends – had been caught in a collapsing real estate market. But he had been overconfident the market would recover and encouraged more backers to invest with him — to buy time and to help cover some of earlier investors' losses.

His timing was several years off.

Prosecutors called the resulting financial implosion Tom Brown's pyramid scheme. *"I knew what I was doing was wrong,"* he says sadly, *"but I was just so sure I could make us all whole again."*

He faced multiple counts of fraud – millions of dollars in value had disappeared—and with it, investors' money.

The man who hadn't known where the jail was located now entered its frightening confines to await trial.

"I knew I would lose everything. I knew I would go to prison. But the thought of my friends' losses was what was unbearable," he recalls. "I didn't know how to handle what was happening to my life. The future was so uncertain, so frightening.

"I committed myself to being a loving presence."

What happens to a loving presence in the company of wily thieves, drug-dealing addicts, violent gang members, and hardened criminals?

That first day in jail, during lunch time, a tattooed bull of a man thundered about the room in a rage. The fearsome giant bellowed at first one man and then another about the "animals" they were eating. They should NOT be eating animal flesh. The thought, let alone the sight, of an outraged vegetarian sermonizing inmates in a jailhouse cafeteria was surreal.

The timid newcomer, too fearful to say a word to any of the surly, rough-looking crowd, finally spoke up when the huge man approached him.

The silver-haired new inmate quietly responded to the yelling man with a question. "Well, then how do you feel about animal crackers?"

The bellowing giant stopped dead and just stared at Tom. Unmanly giggles tittered throughout the room, followed by outright guffaws.

"What did you say to me?" the angry hulk demanded, his voice low and measured.

"How do you feel about animal crackers?" Tom repeated solemnly. An unwilling smile slipped across the giant's face as his joined the laughter filling the room.

"When those men cracked up, releasing their own tensions, perhaps fears, I fully understood the power of laughter to soothe, maybe to heal."

Tom Brown's mission of love launched with laughter.

Tom's friends forgave him despite their enormous losses. But the law demanded justice and restitution. Everything he owned, in fact, would be confiscated and sold to help repay his investors. When it was all gone, he still owed millions in restitution, a debt impossible to ever repay.

While behind bars, Tom earned 50 cents an hour preparing men to take the GED. The conservative white man mixed for the first time in his sheltered life with people of all colors, all religions, all backgrounds, of every economic stratum. He saw first-hand the tragedy of low self-esteem, the lasting impact of poor education. He came to understand how poverty, abandonment, and abuse, nourished by poor judgment and ignorance, could germinate into crime. Most people in prison have committed illegal acts, he saw, but they weren't all the inherently bad people the privileged white man expected to encounter there.

Perhaps it was his age, he speculates, that protected him from the violence he feared, though he did witness violence. Perhaps it was the respect he showed to every man, guard or inmate. Perhaps it was his sense of humor.

Before every class, teacher Tom wrote a joke or pun on the blackboard. The men and he laughed a lot in his classroom. The guards soon began popping in for their own daily chuckles.

His journey to prison was the first he had ever made without a dog at his side. His last dog, a Cocker Spaniel, died shortly before Tom was sentenced. "It was as if he knew he wouldn't be able to come along."

Tom's invisible dog Ralphie was born of the need for a canine companion — and of the desire to create more laughter for his students. In addition to puns on the blackboard, the students began encountering a different drawing of Ralphie every day.

And a jubilant Ralphie decorated every assignment that earned an A. *"Way to go,"* Ralphie might declare. *"Good job!"*

"I'll never forget the day I was handing out diplomas, and one inmate refused to accept his unless I drew Ralphie on the certificate. I told him that a diploma is an official document and that I wasn't sure I should do that."

The man persisted. *"Ralphie got me through this. Ralphie needs to help me celebrate!"* Tom drew a proud Ralphie on the diploma.

Tom walked out of prison an 80-year-old man with $50 in his pocket, every penny earned while inside. He no longer described himself as conservative.

Another Vietnam veteran volunteering with the VA helped him find transitional housing. He was grateful to finally rent a 425-square-foot Section 8 apartment where the manager overlooked his criminal record and his only income, monthly Social Security benefits. Bringing along Ralphie the invisible dog was not a problem.

Reflecting at 90 about his long life, Tom says without hesitation that his 13 years in prison were the most important to him. Not his happy childhood, not his military service, not his wild business successes. Not even traveling the nation to see heroes like Bill Monroe, Willie Nelson, Johnny Cash, or other big-name musicians perform live.

Society's broken men — his fellow human beings of all classes, races, and colors behind bars had made him a wiser man, a better human being able to see beyond society's surface. He became filled with compassion, love — and gratitude. He lives in gratitude today, he says.

Little has changed in his tiny apartment. Modest VA disability benefits now help a bit financially. Ralphie's family has grown with the addition of stuffed dogs Tom's many admirers have gifted him.

"When you have nothing and are living in gratitude," he says, "you realize that even a little is enough."

Tom continues to build a legacy of love, laughter, and gratitude. The changed lives of freed men whom he helped in prison, many still in contact with him, might say his legacy is even greater than that.

Tom Brown has 1000 Facebook friends whom he regales daily with silly puns peppered with thoughtful essays. He loves it when friends pun back and play word games with him. He will accept your friend request if you ask

Ralphie the Dog has his own page, too.

Betsy Brill

Betsy Brill on her age: among the first to receive the polio vaccine in the 1950s and possibly the most eager for COVID-19 vaccines in 2021-22. She's a former journalist, editor, and publication designer. With two women friends, Betsy co-founded HandUp Congo, a tiny non-profit aiding women in the Democratic Republic of Congo. She is an aspiring clay sculptor.

Betsy lives in San Francisco, southern France, and sometimes in Scottsdale, Arizona, where her daughter resides. She and her family have adopted Tom Brown, who advises them to blow bubbles with a straw if chocolate in an iced mocha is not well mixed.

www.handupcongo.org
www.facebook.com/betsybrill
www.ourplaceinprovence.com
Betsyb123@mac.com
PO Box 15306, San Francisco, CA 94115

Scan the QR code with your smartphone or go to:
https://youtu.be/cKcZjphG6Og

A Tree-Based Ego Check

By Brandon Adams

"Someone is sitting in the shade today because someone planted a tree a long time ago."

~ Warren Buffet

Chapter 5

A Tree-Based Ego Check

By Brandon Adams

The Falcon Chair edged toward the top of the hill, slowing down to gently drop us off on our second run of the day. Andrew, Greg, and I had been snowboarding at Big White the past two days and were getting our last runs in before we needed to pack up and head home. I was eighteen years old, mostly fearless, and invincible. Andrew's dad was driving us back and needed us to be ready to go at noon.

The chair was slow at the top. Instead of giving us the shove necessary to glide away smoothly, it nearly stopped, requiring us to awkwardly scoot ourselves out of the way before another chair load was ready to offload. We weren't about that slow nonsense; we had a need for speed.

We sat down, strapped in, stood up, and took off. The snow was fast, and some of our turns revealed layers of ice underneath. Andrew led, Greg was behind him, and I was behind Greg. This part of the mountain had many little bumps, and we whooped and yelled as we popped off of them, celebrating every inch of air.

We dropped down into a little valley in the run and popped out, gathering more speed. I pitched forward, digging the edge of my board into the snow to execute a turn. I'd done these thousands of times, but it didn't work this time. I was on a sheet of ice.

There was also a tree in front of me, and I was on a collision course.

Within a second or so, I'd assessed that the tree didn't look so big, I had no chance of changing direction, and my only option was to brace for impact. I thought I'd probably break the tree, but it couldn't be helped. It was a pine, about six feet tall.

I curled up, collided, and entered a world of bizarre sensations. I hit the small of my back square on the tree trunk. It felt like my entire body was a funny bone. I thought maybe I'd paralyzed myself, that I might die, and that I hadn't even gotten a girlfriend yet. My instincts turned to screaming. I wasn't yet in any pain. I think my subconscious just needed to yell out for help, and the best way was apparently high-pitched girlish shrieking.

Once I heard my friends yelling back, I stopped screaming and checked myself out. I'd landed on my side, with my back to the tree, together making an upside-down capital T. I tried to reposition myself onto my back and was relieved to find that I was able to move at all. As I moved, I saw that my left leg had moved twice. Once, I shifted my torso, and then again, as if the lower bit of it forgot to move and struggled to catch up. Legs aren't supposed to move like that. I'd broken my femur.

Greg reached me, and I told him I thought my femur was broken, and he told me it looked super swollen, like a watermelon. He also told me Andrew had gone down the hill to fetch ski patrol.

Greg kept me company. My memory's fuzzy here, but I think we were joking around. I remember him being shocked and repeating that he couldn't believe I had broken my leg. He also ribbed me about my screams, as friends do.

A member of the Ski Patrol arrived with Andrew after about ten minutes. Patrol brought a stretcher on skis that he could tow behind him and a bottle of nitrous oxide. I was in a bit of pain by this point, but not as much as you'd probably expect. Endorphins and adrenaline are powerful painkillers.

Patrol told me I'd probably want the nitrous, and I obliged. He hooked me up with a face mask to inhale the nitrous and got to work.

He started by cutting off my pants. I protested. I'd just gotten them a couple of weeks ago, and this weekend had been my first time wearing them. I asked if he could just slide my pants off instead. He laughed, said he was sorry that he couldn't, and cut through my snow pants and my thermal underwear. I was exposed.

Another ski patrol guy joined the ski patrol guy, and they loaded me onto the stretcher. They explained that it might be a bumpy ride and advised me to breathe deep on the nitrous to counteract the pain. I took some deep breaths, said bye to Greg, and then said "faja" repeatedly, imitating a scene from a movie we'd watched the night before. Greg thought this was hilarious.

Taking deep breaths of the nitrous turned out to be super valuable advice. The bumps were unlike any pain I'd ever felt before, and the nitrous was a massive help. It was even more support once we reached the point where they could transfer me over to a snowmobile, which featured more speed and bumps.

We reached the lodge, and a team of medical professionals was waiting for me. They got me into a bed, hooked me up to an IV, and gave me even better drugs. The pain was no longer a problem. It was present, I was fully aware of it, but it was just pain. Why worry? Even when they set the bone, painful, sure, but not a big deal.

The bigger deal was that the IV replaced a lot of fluids that had escaped my bones and inflated my leg. And my kidneys were filtering that IV fluid, and I had to pee. I informed a nurse, and she retrieved a plastic urinal, and I got to pee in front of the whole team. Again though, nothing to worry about.

The team at the mountain readied me for ambulance transport. I have no memory of the ambulance ride; I'm pretty sure they drugged me past the point of consciousness as a courtesy so that I wouldn't have a memory of all the bumps and switchbacks on the mountain road.

My memory resumes in the hospital. I was in a bed in the hallway. A doctor was giving me options. I had two decisions to make. First, I could stay at this hospital in Canada or be flown back to the states. I talked with my mom on the phone and decided on the states to be closer to home. Second, I could opt for a rod in my leg, which would mean a faster recovery but with major surgery, or let my leg heal on its own. I chose the rod.

I vaguely remember another ambulance ride and being loaded onto a plane. Then time skipped, and I was recovering in a hospital bed in Harborview Medical Center in Seattle.

I'm grateful to my friends and the strangers that pitched in to help me. Without my friends, I might've frozen to death. The ski patrol and medical professionals ensured that I'd survive, make a full recovery, and walk slowly a few weeks later. It's dangerous to go alone.

Brandon Adams

Brandon works as a site reliability engineer for a Silicon Valley startup.

He grew up in Washington state, where he now lives with his beautiful wife, Lulu. They are expecting their first child in early 2022.

A Different Kind of Cowboy

By Brian Dygert

"There is something about the outside of a horse that is good for the inside of a man."

~ Winston Churchill

Chapter 6

A Different Kind of Cowboy

By Brian Dygert

Trying to gain admission to veterinary school – what a process! Seventy-five seats each year for an admission class and about 15 of them become part of a competitive pool of hundreds applying. I was on the alternate list two years in a row and found myself on the hillside with my dog, watching horses in the pasture pondering what was next. Admission to veterinary school was not in my control. It didn't matter how hard or how bad I was willing to work at it, go or no go was in the hands of a committee. That was a humbling ride.

While in undergraduate school, I spent all my time at the university farm with the few horses and beef cattle herds available. I was hanging around the North Carolina Quarter Horse Association since Raleigh had the new Jim Hunt Horse Complex being built there. The quarter horse industry was buzzing with activity. Opportunities were being pursued as the first National Reining Horse Association Derby event was held in Dorton Arena in Raleigh, North Carolina in 1983.

The first reining futurity prize check was guaranteed to be $100,000. I was young and dreaming of what could be; just my dog and me, wanting to compete on reining horses. Could I make a living? Two colleagues and acquaintances were my age. Rick Weaver, from Ohio, won the reining futurity in 1982 as an assistant trainer. Craig Johnson, from Iowa, won the first $100,000 guarantee in 1983. The thought still wouldn't leave my mind. Could a guy make a living riding reining horses in the second half of the 20th century in America?

A person can't go to school for this because the horse is the teacher. A mentor can lead you and interpret what the horse is saying, which greatly speeds up training and is much more fun. Without it, people can get hurt. We think and communicate like people, but you have to change to think and communicate like a horse!

The words my father spoke to me on the phone from Western New York to North Carolina, using old-fashioned landlines, and long-distance toll fees are unforgettable. His words boiled down to this, "Son, it's a hard life. Gotta ride. Onward. It's a one-way trail."

My mother was the greatest woman I have ever known. I still miss her. "Embrace the moment, stay humble and keep riding. Do it right." The wisdom of those in front of us, like a horse – listen, embrace, and learn. It's a great ride!

I became a certified licensed official in 1985 for reining horses and gained certification to the FEI level (International Equestrian Federation, teacher, and official). I retired from my license in 2020.

We will never know it all. The lessons to be learned lie at our feet, under our seats, in our hands, and in the mirror; but how ignorant and egotistical we get. I believe the biggest question is the wisdom of asking, "What don't I know?" Here is the humbling moment of forward movement. When in doubt, spend more time with the horse. The horse may tell you, or just calm your mind, and help you find the answer. Take the time to listen, embrace, and learn.

It's early 1997, months after riding an exhibition in the 1996 Olympics, and I got a phone call from a politician in North Carolina. The politician asked if I would be interested in helping build a new horse show complex, market it, and get it operational. It earned my respect for the role and responsibility of elected leaders and politicians. As a young wise guy, thinking I already knew it all, how wrong I was and continue to be. We all need a little bit of humbling.

I saw two huge opportunities: learning from the wisdom of senior statesmen and creating a new advanced opportunity for the horse show world. A new trail, saddle up, let's ride. The Senator Bob Martin Eastern Agricultural Center not only thrived but also became a favorite and leading facility to many horse people on the east coast that they still enjoy and utilize to this day. That Center made another stride forward for the industry and catalyzed economic change.

In 2007, I got a strange phone call from North Carolina asking if I might be interested in working for the City of Scottsdale to advance the vision for WestWorld and the equine industry.

So, my wife and I moved to Scottsdale, Arizona and I became a city employee. We expanded WestWorld with a multi-million-dollar capital investment business plan and transformed a seasonal part-time facility into a year-round major venue with climate control on the national platform.

WestWorld hosted the largest major International Arabian horse show, owned and produced by the Arabian Horse Association of Arizona.

WestWorld hosted the largest Quarter Horse Circuit in the country, owned and produced by the Arizona Quarter Horse Association.

WestWorld hosted the largest qualifying event in the sport of reining, the Cactus Classic Reining and Run for the Million qualifier, produced by Brumley Management Group.

WestWorld created a new business relationship with the National Reined Cowhorse Association (NRCHA). They own and produce

The NRCHA DT Horses Western Derby. This national event is two weeks in June.

Forty years later, I am now in my last chapter, still riding because the horses never let me down. They keep me humble.

What sport do you know of that has men and women competing on absolutely equal grounds? The horse only cares about the state of your heart, soul, and mind.

The horse lives on his own timetable no matter what. Listen, embrace, and learn. The older horses can be the best teachers! Learn from them.

I find myself in the second half of my career doing some unorthodox projects. I'm still learning. Yes, of course, my love for the quarter horse and the sport of reining supersedes all the others, but my love and appreciation for what the "horse" offers to people is my real pursuit in this last chapter of my life. Taking a non-essential, "hobby" industry, the modern horse industry, and exposing it to the public.

Find a horse and put him or her in your life and the life of your children and grandchildren. A horse will teach you and guide you and make you a better person. Just listen, embrace, and learn. Learn to communicate "horse" and just watch. Your time with a horse will make you a better person in every way and will even positively affect those around you!

When we are done, did we make a difference with those we rode with? The horses have my answer – ask them!

May God continue to bless us all with our horses!

Brian Dygert

Brian Dygert, Scottsdale's general manager at WestWorld, was inducted into the League of Agricultural and Equine Centers Hall of Fame in January 2022.

Born in 1959 in Illinois, Brian grew up in Western New York as the son of a veterinarian and the grandson of a Standardbred horseman. Brian has made an entire career and lifestyle around the reining horse business.

Brian started his business in 1986 as a horse breeding, training, and coaching facility. The business has transformed to become an event production entity primarily focused on the horse show industry.

Horses change lives and will love unconditionally.

CONTACT:
bdygertaz@gmail.com

Scan the QR code with your smartphone or go to:
https://youtu.be/_KM87mMYtXg

Legacy of a Genius

By Cat Parenti

There will be a day.
That day I will understand why civilization,
Is feminine...
And why poetry is feminine
And why love letters are feminine
And why women,
When they're in love
Like the sparrow going to the light
Turn into flames...

~ Nazar Qabani, Afghan Poet

Chapter 7

Legacy of a Genius

By Cat Parenti

"Grandma" Chandra is a young woman who, although severely physically handicapped, has significantly changed many lives worldwide. Born to an Afghan nobleman who practiced the miracles of Sufi Islamism, she received his gifts in utero upon his passing. The way of the Sufis is a humble, powerful, prayerful path strewn with miracles. The Muslims revere Jesus Christ, Moses, and Muhammad as great prophets and believe in the powers of Mother Mary, the Angels, and high adepts like Grandma Chandra to help humanity. The Muslims call her "*Shaykha*" Chandra, a loose translation of an adept.

Chandra arrived on this Earth as a fully awakened being. The title "grandma" was given to her by the late Chief Golden Light Eagle of the Yankton Sioux of South Dakota when he adopted her as an honorary member of his tribe. The titles of "grandmother" and "grandfather" are given to those with wisdom and not necessarily due to age. She traveled around the U.S. with the Chief giving many presentations, helping him with his mission to unite Native Americans with all groups of people through his native teachings based on the principle that "we are all one." Eagle called Grandma a "very powerful teacher."

Chandra created her current business at age sixteen. Gr. Chandra's Global Spiritual Healing LLC. is based upon the age-old belief that all diseases or disorders come from pre-birth contracts which we choose to experience and/or unresolved emotional issues that block our true Path to Ascension. Her mission in this lifetime is to help those who are ready to release "all that no longer serves them." Nonverbal and with limited use of her hands, Chandra has honed her cognitive brain to laser sharpness. She is clairvoyant, clairaudient, clairsentient and has access to the Akashic Records. This allows her to heal and help people nationally and internationally by using her mind.

She says, "Change your mind, change your life." She can read Auras from the Quantum Light Field and heals through the Light Codes and frequencies within her Holographic Fractal videos, her Sacred Geometric Forms, high vibrational essential oils from the Sufi Masters of Afghanistan, apps, and the green healing laser. All her tools which are personally encoded for each client, make changes at the cellular level allowing people to move forward on their spiritual path, creating a better life. Since age nine, Chandra's life has been one of service to humanity.

Grandma's Melchizedek Vortex pendant is a powerful tool that works within the Divine Flow of Creation, allowing your intentions to manifest in alignment with God/Creator/Source's Plan. Grandma says, "This is how Creator intended for you to manifest and create. Your 3D programming has taken you off this path. The Melchizedek Vortex Pendant will move you out of 3D 'in your head' thinking so you can connect with your intuition and move into the Divine Flow of Creation. In addition, the Pendant can keep your Biological Age at the Master Number 33. This number indicates the ability to manifest your gifts of gentleness and purity, furthering you on your Path to Ascension. It can also protect you from past, and future viruses, bacteria, and fungi as well as clear past, present, and future lives."

Grandma is an Ascended Master who is multi-dimensional, meaning that she can appear simultaneously in many places on Earth and other realms. Her clients report that she appears in the form of a dolphin, a whale, or an over seven-foot tall, beautiful woman. Her most common communication is telepathy, sometimes in Light Language, although Grandma uses human translators for readings. Check out her website to meet Grandma's team. www.GrandmaChandra.com

She is clairvoyant, clairaudient and clairsentient and has access to the Akashic Records.

The crowning glory of her life is the legacy of a physical retreat center here in Bisbee, Arizona, for wholistic healers. Everybody needs a break! Gr. Chandra's Blue Lotus Healing Sanctuary LLC. will open in 2023. She aims to recreate the ancient Afghan *Shafkhana healing house* serving healers with various wholistic modalities, such as acupuncture, cranial/sacral, hydrotherapy, chakra balancing, color healing, etc. We all need a getaway, especially healers who work 24/7 to help others. We are looking for a property with one to two acres to have a garden, fruit trees, chickens, a pool, and a hot tub. We will build casitas out of earth-friendly material to house the healers. The Center will also benefit the local community by using local restaurants and local certified practitioners to perform the therapies.

Grandma can reach into the universe to those who are suffering and help them. We receive many phone calls and emails from all over the world, thanking her for her healings and blessings. Grandma finds them through the double or triple numbers in their birth dates. She said that these people, she has thousands of clients, have contracted to work with her for Planetary Ascension in this lifetime. Besides giving homework to clients, she has a FREE FOREVER email service for those who have had a full reading with her.

After working with Grandma, here are some messages sent to her.

> *"Thank you, thank you so much for this session - So very grateful, and I have a lot to "digest"! So many things to help me - I am blown away by your care!" Jane*

"So grateful in deep inner gratitude in watching your short video clips. They bring so much deep inner being and happy peace of existence to me." Marianne

"With great humility, I thank you for the Forgiveness meditation. I used it just a few minutes ago, and it was quite profound. My heart was burning, and my 6th Chakra was vibrating. I didn't realize how many people I needed to forgive…including myself. I made a list, and while working with the people on the list, others came up. It was wonderful…this way, I know I didn't forget anyone. I thought I had forgiven people through the years… but I guess it was a "mental exercise" rather than a heartfelt forgiveness." Anna

Cat Parenti

Cat Parenti is a transplanted Brooklynite, who graduated from Fordham University, lived in Afghanistan, survived the political twists of Afghan politics from King Zahir Shah through the rise of the Taliban.

Cat started a successful export business selling Afghan clothing and jewelry in America, has given many presentations including the U.N., and taught Afghan cooking. Subsequently, she became the Director of the Afghanistan Foundation, personally delivering humanitarian aid inside Afghanistan, and honored by Hillary Clinton. Cat authored 5 books on Afghanistan, one in the Smithsonian Library.

Cat Parenti, Author
Afghanistan: A Memoir from Brooklyn to Kabul*
Director of the Afghanistan Foundation
cat.parenti@gmail.com
520-508-0211
*Amazon bestseller
www.CatParenti.com
www.GrandmaChandra.com

Finding Freedom in Prison

By Charles Tom Brown

*"When you have nothing and are living in gratitude,
you realize that even a little is enough."*

~ Charles Tom Brown

Chapter 8

Finding Freedom in Prison

By Charles Tom Brown

For most of my life, my identity depended on an endless collection of things to prop it up: my name, my "biography," my partners, home, job, bank balance... It was on their fragile and temporary support that I relied upon for my security.

When I went to prison, I was stripped of everything that had composed my identity.

Without the familiar props, I had to focus on myself, a person I did not know, an unnerving stranger with whom I had been living but never really wanted to meet. I had filled my days with countless distractions and activities to ensure I would not be left in silence with this stranger.

I finally met that stranger in a prison cell. No longer could I use my computer, my TV, and every gadget and activity I could think of to divert my attention. All that was left for me to do was face myself.

At long last, layer after layer of resistances and denials were peeled away, and what was left was a tenderness I had not known before. When I reached my core, I felt everything in a new and deeper way.

I learned that seeing one's own unwanted behaviors and claiming them, declaring them, and owning them is a first step many never take. It's too painful.

Perhaps sharing our painful experiences can help others see themselves. And they, too, will move closer to healing. When we lay our life open and allow our flaws and frailties to be known, our magnificence shines through, too, and through our example, others are healed. Through sharing our pain, others are relieved of theirs. Through our experience, others have hope.

Cries of the Heart

As a teacher's aide in the Arizona prison system, I helped students to prepare for their GED essay requirements. They were given the format and topic for their essay. One topic was "If you could have one wish, what would it be?" I assumed that most would be wishes to get out of prison or something of that nature. Instead, many were cries of the heart… cries to love and be loved.

One essay stated, "If I could have one wish, I would wish for a letter from my mother. She hasn't written to me in years, and it would mean so much to me to get a letter from her."

Another inmate's two-year-old daughter was living with foster parents. His wish would be to hear his daughter on the phone. I told him that she wouldn't be able to say much at the age of two. He replied, "I just want to hear the sound of her voice."

As I read these essays, I was reminded that we never lose our deep basic need to connect with the soulfulness of each other's hearts. Each of us has a story to tell, and we're traveling our personal road of transformation. Listening to the stories of others and the cries of their hearts is a kind of water that breaks the fever of our isolation.

If we listen closely enough, we are soothed into remembering our common name.

I believe that expressing our truth releases light and warmth. It's the way our spirit shines. Those essay writers were my medicine. And I was theirs. We are members of a broken whole. And we will heal... a stitch, a song, a cry at a time.

Personal Prisons

Mohini, a white tiger, spent years pacing back and forth in her twelve-by-twelve-foot cage in the Washington, D.C., National Zoo. Eventually, a natural habitat was created for her. Covering several acres, it had hills, trees, a pond, and a variety of vegetation. With excitement and anticipation, the staff released Mohini into her new, expansive environment. The tiger immediately sought refuge in a corner of the compound. There she lived for the remainder of her life, pacing back and forth in an area measuring twelve-by-twelve feet.

Some prisons are built with concrete, steel, and razor wire. Others are built in the dungeons of our minds. Though freedom is possible, we often pass our years trapped in the same old patterns. We cage ourselves into our self-imposed prisons with self-judgment and anxiety. Then, with the passing of time, we, like Mohini, grow incapable of accessing the freedom and peace that is our birthright.

However, life is continually calling us to become more, to journey into the wilderness, and face the truth of our lives. In my case, the shell of my life had to be softened, broken down even, by the experience of going to prison before the moment of truth could appear. I needed to be humbled, cooked in the tears of loss, for any deeper life to emerge.

A fresh life requires a death of some kind; otherwise, it is nothing new but rather a shuffling of the same old deck. We die is an outworn way of being in the world. We are no longer who we thought we were.

On the deepest level, this journey of awakening opens us to the innermost center of love. Love creates its own freedom from imprisonment, has its own direction, moves according to its own rhythm, and makes its own music.

A Free Spirit

The signs in the prison visitation room stated the many restrictions. Don't do this. Don't do that. Dress a certain way. Act a certain way.

However, in the midst of all of this, a free spirit was on the loose.

A young boy, perhaps three or four years old, decided to have fun with the dominoes his dad was trying to put into a container. He picked up handfuls of them and gleefully began throwing them in the air. The more the adults tried to gather up the dominoes and get him to stop, the more fun he had.

As I watched this, I thought of some things I'd like to say to this little fellow:

Keep laughing and giggling when you're surprised and delighted; it offers our ears the music of grace.

Remain excited at the discovery of dominoes; it tells us there is significance in small things when our eyes have become too focused on the big things.

Play with other children on playgrounds; it shows us that all people of all backgrounds can meet each other with open arms.

Keep talking to the dogs and cats and pigeons and ducks; it reminds us that the spirit is present in all living things.

You have the gift of innocence, of dreams. When we see you laughing and playing, our spirits take wing. When we lift you and hold you, we are consecrating a world of hope.

You are hope when our hope has dimmed. You are joy when our hearts are heavy. In you, we see the world as we dream it could be.

For you remind us what it means to be alive.

Charles Tom Brown

Tom Brown was a successful real estate investor when in the 1990s, the value of his and his backers' investments faltered with the market.

He recruited new investors; certain a coming upswing would make everyone whole and more.

What prosecutors called his Ponzi Scheme collapsed. At 67 years old, Tom went to prison, where he spent 13 years.

He lost everything—and committed the rest of his life to become "a loving presence" to others. Now 90 years old, Tom lives on Social Security and VA disability benefits in a tiny studio apartment.

www.facebook.com/charlestombrown
www.charlestombrown.wordpress.com

Scan the QR code with your smartphone or go to:
https://youtu.be/pu5xPStAo0Q

Uncle

By Chris G. Weisling

*"By small and simple things are great
things brought to pass."*

~ Alma the Younger, about 74 B.C.

Chapter 9

Uncle

By Chris G. Weisling

I was taught the Golden Wisdom of Love and the profound legacies it can have on individuals and families, in some cases stretching across generations in the positive effects it can have, by my Uncle.

Uncle was born John Hubert Bowman on 12/17/1912 in Dexter, Chaves Co., New Mexico. He was the second of three children and was the older brother of my mother. From my earliest memories, I remember Uncle's kindness and love, not only to me but to almost everyone. Every life he touched was a little bit better, a little bit kinder, and a little bit happier for having known him.

Uncle was 12 years older than mom, and he had always spoiled her rotten. Uncle grew up initially on ranches in Western New Mexico and Eastern Arizona. The family moved to Glendale, Arizona when he was about 10 years old; that is where mom was born. Uncle dropped out of high school at the end of his junior year, it was the roaring 20's, and he thought he knew all he needed to know. He soon found out that wasn't the case. When he was about 19 years old, he returned to high school and graduated. He then enlisted in the U.S. Army and was trained as a radio operator and achieved the rank of sergeant before his enlistment ended. By then the family had moved to Clifton, Arizona in Greenlee County. He took a job with Phelps-Dodge Corporation which operated a large open pit copper mine in Morenci, just up the hill from Clifton. He became a journeyman electrician.

Then along came World War II. Being a journeyman electrician for a large copper mine made Uncle exempt from the draft. However, he had an agreement with his best friend Fergie Ferguson, that if one of them was drafted the other would volunteer. Fergie was drafted, so Uncle volunteer to re-enlist. Because of his prior service, he went back in as a staff sergeant. Both Uncle and Fergie landed on Omaha Beach on D-Day and were later assigned to General Patton's 3rd Armored Division.

During the Battle of the Bulge, Uncle was with the forces sent to relieve the besieged 101st Airborne Division in Bastogne. Uncle's company came under heavy enemy shelling by German 88-millimeter guns. Despite the danger from the numerous shells exploding around him, Uncle stayed on his radio and redirecting U.S. Artillery until the enemy guns were destroyed. Uncle received the Bronze Star for Valor for his actions that day. As the war drew to a close and they entered Germany, Uncle and his company were among the U.S. Troops that liberated the Buchwald Concentration Camp. He would not talk very much about the war, most veterans who have experience combat don't. But he had many photographs of the horrors they found at Buchwald.

After the war, Uncle returned to Clifton, where he was elected Clerk of the Superior Court for Greenlee County. He also paid for Mom to attend Arizona State College (later Arizona State University) where she met my Dad, a recently discharged Army Air Corp Pilot, who was attending College on the G.I. Bill. My parents graduated from Arizona State University in 1950 and moved to Eastern Arizona where they accepted teaching positions.

Uncle became the owner/operator of a small bar and grill in Duncan during the 1950's but he wanted more out of life. At age 44, he began work on his bachelor's degree in education at Western New Mexico University in Silver City, NM. Each week he would commute the 90 plus miles from Duncan, AZ to Silver City. In May 1960 he received his bachelor's degree in education. The following fall he began his teaching career teaching 5th grade at Duncan Elementary School.

While he enjoyed teaching, he was not sure that was his true calling. He then enrolled in the master's degree program for guidance and counseling at Western New Mexico University and received his master's degree. Uncle was then promoted to Guidance Counselor at Duncan High School. In this position Uncle found his true destiny. Over the next twenty years he touched the lives of thousands of young men and women. I do not have space in this chapter to give a full accounting of all the lives he touched. So, I will include a few that personally touched my life and my heart.

The first was a scrawny boy, a few years behind me in school. I remember that he was always getting into fights, chronically tardy, and most teachers considered him a "bad" student. Uncle took a special interest in this boy and began to counsel him. I remember on many occasions the counseling sessions began at a local café, where Uncle bought him breakfast. I later learned that this boy had a terrible home life. His father was an abusive alcoholic, and his mother was absent from the home. The reason he was so scrawny was because he only got to eat at school. Uncle made arrangements for him to get breakfasts at school, this was before our current free and reduced breakfast and lunch programs. Uncle also began to tutor him and his grades dramatically improved.

I went off to college and lost track of this young man. Then I came home to visit my parents. To my great surprise I ran into this young man, now grown and a law enforcement officer. We talked for a little while and he told me, "If it had not been for Mr. Bowman, I would be dead or in prison. He helped me learn to deal with my anger and he taught me the value of education. I learn to love learning and went on to get my A.A. degree EAC in Law Enforcement. I truly love your Uncle for all he did for me."

In a time before FERPA, HIPAA and other federal regulations that schools have to deal with, a Guidance Counselor could submit students' names for scholarships and grants for which they qualified. Something that Uncle loved to do was to help good students obtain the means to go to college. However, in a small community where many students were first time high school graduates, this dream seemed so far out of reach for them that they would not even apply. So, Uncle being who he was, would apply on their behalf's. Then a few weeks before graduation he would call the student to his office and ask them where they would like to go to college. Their replies were, "Oh, Mr. Bowman, you know that my parents can't afford to send me to college." Uncle would then present them with their combination of scholarships and grant awards that covered all the costs of their college or university education. At this point most of them broke into tears. Not surprisingly, many of these students went into education, but whatever they got their degree in, they all thanked Uncle for making it possible for them. He being the humble man that he was, would always say, "I just filled out the paperwork, you did all the work yourself."

Uncle passed away 09/29/1986, but the golden wisdom of love and the legacy that it left has transcended several generations of his family and the families of those whose lives he touched.

Chris G. Weisling

Chris is a 2nd generation Arizonan, born and raised in Southeastern Arizona. He attended Arizona State University, where he earned both a B.S. in psychology, and an M.Ed. in higher and adult education. He also earned a J.D. from Ohio Northern University, College of Law.

He served as a law enforcement officer in Arizona for 17 years., he also practiced law, and has been an educator at the high school and college levels. For the past 15 years, he has worked in public mental health, the last 10 years as a compliance/privacy officer for a healthcare company in Southern Arizona.

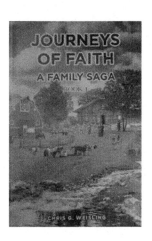

Journeys of Faith – A Family Saga
http://covenantbooks.com/
books/?book=journeys-of-faith-a-family-saga-book-1
Available on Amazon, Barnes & Nobles, iTunes, and Walmart.com
Website: www.weislingassociatesllc.com
Email: ArmyDad5619@gmail.com
Phone: 928-303-4188

Scan the QR code with your
smartphone or go to:
https://youtu.be/6FBB_e8eSBc

Healing Our Wholeness

by Cynthia Young

"I've learned that loving yourself requires a courage unlike any other. It requires us to believe in and stay loyal to something no one else can see that keeps us in the world-our own self-worth."

~ Mark Nepo

Chapter 10

Healing Our Wholeness

By Cynthia Young

Four words changed the direction of my life: "Get up and walk," spoken by my mother as I struggled to steady myself on the parallel bars after suffering a stroke at age six. The bright traffic against the night sky made my terror worse as we crossed the Tobin Bridge in Boston. The cool, clear September night became the dark that swallowed up the childhood that existed before the left side of my body stopped moving. I was dying. A tiny body, almost limp in my mother's arms, wrapped in a brown granny square blanket.

I've told this story countless times, how they said I'd never walk or go to school; their determination to make me a sad victim. The larger story is the magic of what was given back. A great portal of human connection opened to allow me to have an elevated bond, intense compassion, and empathy for others and myself as the journey through life unfolded.

There are moments during my multi-week hospital stay that I don't recall. What I remember is feeling my left leg move again for the first time. I remember I heard a small child crying for his mom outside my hospital room and wanting to transcend my own paralyzed body to somehow get to him to give comfort. "What do you need to make you feel safe?" Trauma is not the event that happened to you but your memory of it and your body's response to it. Trauma stays with us because our body doesn't get a chance to finish taking care of that threat. My body feels like it's been in constant threat for 48 years.

I stood there fascinated and enthralled by the clanging sound of the brass elevator door crashing, being closed by a porter in the old city building on Harrison Avenue. The gold buttons on his bright white blazer matched the door. I was holding my mom's hand as we made our way down the hallway to get my first AFO.

Ankle foot orthosis ("AFO") is a custom-built brace that is always worn on the foot or lower leg. It surrounds the foot and controls how much the ankle and foot can move. Simultaneously, it keeps both of them in a natural position to help someone walk or stand.

The cold wetness of the plaster of Paris on my skin was in contrast to the metallic saw that cut the newly-shaped mold off my leg. I swore that buzzsaw would cut off my leg, so I held my breath. I had to learn to walk again. The brace allowed my ankle to be supported but sharply cut my connection to being included socially with my peers.

My stroke happened the night before the first day of first grade. After several months, I returned to school in a wheelchair and was tutored in order to keep up with my classmates. The stroke affected my body, but not my intelligence, my movement, or my soul. I became a great storyteller about what happened. That moment of storytelling was the first breach of authenticity. I lied so I could survive.

I could easily have died that night. That night, the ischemia diverted my life's path onto a road that would have a far greater impact. Mind and spirit could have collapsed after the body revolted. The blood clot launched by the tearing and ripping of my carotid artery brought me inches from being in the unseen. The things my body does now are because it remembers how it needed to survive.

It was a few years later when someone stood next to me at the top of the metal and wood slide, her red hair and freckles gleaming in the April sun, and said, "My mom says you're a cripple." In that split second, I felt every sharp thrust of the wood and hot metal that slide was made of. My reaction, which was pure sadness and isolation, is something my body hasn't forgotten. I carry it with me even though I am 54 and know that my classmate, a 10-year-old girl, was probably not responsible for what she said. By acknowledging it and the countless other incidents of staring, cruel questions, and physical bullying, I can be compassionate with myself. I recognize that my body is different and that it is miserable on days when I feel spasticity and pain, and that I am worthy of treating myself with kindness. I learned to walk and thrive — a gift that clapped back at the medical doubters. Divine intervention had been orchestrated.

Do you want to have a more open heart? Practice moments of compassion for others. My story is paved with steppingstones of being different. I had no choice but to set myself apart. Yet the river that always flowed through each experience was that I saw the loneliness in every bully, the frustration and overwork of every teacher who made fun of me, the curiosity and self-questioning from every person who stared and asked, "What's wrong with your arm?" Ultimately, they were all navigating their own darkness they hadn't yet faced.

I felt the darkness. I could feel sad about them saying hurtful things, annihilated sometimes, but that didn't compare to the isolation they were feeling themselves. Hurt people hurt the most. Revenge is an empty promise; it's like walking toward a well, dying of thirst, only to find sand and grass have grown over the opening. You're the only one suffering. We can set boundaries and practice self-preservation, but there's nothing to be gained by hurting someone more than they already hurt. It's our human responsibility to listen, be present, and be accepting of the fact that there are things we don't love about ourselves. We hurl the unlovable things at each other in an attempt to run from our own pain.

Something was removed, but something was added back, tenfold. I am still here through days of pain and joy. Why? To be whole. To reconnect the mind, body, and spirit and show others how to feel safe in their environment.

I now practice Feng Shui in the Southwest, a LONG way from that big, busy, paint-chipped Boston Hospital. At six years old, I had never before heard busy traffic on a city street. Today, strangers welcome me into their homes to share their stories. We look at how their experiences and survival show up in their space. I get to see their accomplishments, joys, and experiences that are ingrained in the environment around them. I get to feel the whisper of intentions and dreams growing. Feng Shui means having the honor of bearing witness to others' stories and responding with, "You're just like me." We help each other heal the things we don't love, the things we keep hidden and show no one. We take each other into our wounds to wrap, console, celebrate, and feel safe. Those things in your soul, those things in your home – they're ready to feel the water and be supported by the wind. They are ready to expand and be expressed.

In that energy, as Divinely chosen witnesses, we heal each other into being.

Cynthia Young

Cynthia Young is a Boston-born native now living in Surprise, Arizona. She is a Feng Shui practitioner and Trauma Support specialist. She lives a life philosophy based on balanced wellness. Cynthia's history as a pediatric stroke survivor allows her to help others create a regulated, safe environment and celebrate self-compassion as medicine.

The past traumas that we continue to experience show up in our living spaces as familiar vehicles of comfort. Wind and water support their integration into healthy wholeness. Through Feng Shui, we can live the invitation of self-compassion and healing and shift the energy toward joyful living.

Links to Cynthia's Work and Contact Info:

https://asteyastudios.com
https://www.instagram.com/asteyastudios_feng_shui

cynthiayoung.az@gmail.com
(978) 771-1002

Scan the QR code with your smartphone or go to:
https://youtu.be/G0p7-pmysuU

Welcome to My World

By Florine Duffield

"Let Us Not Take Ourselves Too Seriously.
None of Us Has a Monopoly on Wisdom."

~ Queen Elizabeth II

Chapter 11

Welcome to My World

By Florine Duffield

After graduating from high school in 1967, I moved to New York City, throwing myself into a show business career: modeling, TV and film actor, nightclub singer, and college student.

In 1968, my mother came to visit from Colorado. I rented a 2-room suite at the Hotel Arlington on 25th Street, built by the infamous architect Stanford White, murdered by a jealous husband. Cost for suite $50 a week: What I earned in a one-hour modeling session would cover my monthly expenses.

John Cabore lived in the room next door and kept his door open.

I wandered into a wonderland that changed my life. When I looked through John's portfolio, I realized I was in the company of a renowned artist. He had not painted in years. He was devastated by the death of his wife; lost everything; had a pacemaker due to a heart attack. John smoked and drank copious amounts of Vodka.

We became close friends; he was a father figure/teacher. I bought art supplies, modeled for him, and monitored his diet. He was able to create a huge body of work during the next ten years.

Overview of John Cabore:
Fashion Artist / Illustrator / Portrait Artist / Educator

Born 6 May 1914, Larksville, PA
Passed: New York City 1980

During WWII 1941-1945, John was in Military Intelligence – at MacDill Army Base in Florida. He traveled the world as a writer/artist for AP, UP, and Intelligence, making portraits of high-ranking foreign military figures and magnificent murals for the officers' clubs.

John was a prominent fashion artist and commercial illustrator in NYC during the 1940s – 1960s for the city's high-end department stores: Saks, Bergdorf Goodman, and Bonwit Teller. He illustrated for major magazines and anatomy for textbooks.

He was one of the original instructors at the School of Visual Arts, founded in 1947 by Silas Rhodes and Burne Hogarth, the Tarzan illustrator.

John's drinking buddies included Jackson Pollack (the father of Abstract Expressionism), Howard Purcell, and Andrew Palencar. Howard Purcell was a well-known illustrator of the comic book giant DC. In Howard Purcell's own words, "John Cabore was one of the best damn artists he had ever run into" Andy Palencar saw John's painting at the Art Students League displayed as an example of an "Excellent Portrait Painting." Andy describes John Cabore as "One of the greatest living artists. "

The first time Kay and John met was in a stuck elevator on a Saturday afternoon. They were moving into a new apartment building on the same floor, as it turned out. Their bags from the shops were loaded with scotch whiskey. By the time they were rescued 90 minutes later, they were on the floor, both plastered. She was so beautiful; he had to have her. That started his doom.

Kay Silver was a stage actor who performed with Sophie Tucker. Richard Rogers of the Rogers & Hammerstein fame – "Oklahoma!" jump-started Kay's career by placing her in the lead for the play's first road trip.

GOLDEN WISDOM OF LOVE LEGENDS & LEGACIES

Once married, Kay and John lived on Fifth Avenue in NYC, socialized with the glamorous celebrities – living the life! Sadly, Kay Silver died from brain cancer; there was no cure for her. John was devastated, disappeared from life, and produced no work - his students could not find him.

His only income was a pension from the Government. He injured his back jumping out of a window while serving with Intelligence during WWII.

Memories of John Cabore

John took me to MOMA (the Museum of Modern Art). Monet's "Water Lilies" room was fifty feet long, or so it seemed to my young eyes. John described this magnificent piece to me with tears rolling down his face, choking with emotion. He had such a passion and reverence for art, and he passed that on to me. In the creative arts, you become lost; little else matters.

My life is my work; my work is my life.

I was not a drinker. My mother loved to party, so when she came to visit, the two of them went wild. During mother's visits, we saw all the top shows, and her favorite was the Christmas show at Radio City Music Hall.

John was working on a painting of me; he did not like the way it was progressing; he got drunk and threw it out the 10th-floor window. For all his bluster and passion, he never once made me feel uncomfortable. He treated me with respect and tenderness, more like a daughter.

John Cabore ignited my interest in healthful living, still alive in me today. He had a Ph.D. in anatomy and predicted the harmful side effects of the medications and food on the market during that time.

At that time, I became more interested in being on the other side of the camera. I studied lighting and the magic of the darkroom with the top photographers. I switched my major from music to photography.

He told me I was intelligent, kind, determined – that I could do anything I set my mind & heart to. You cannot create in a vacuum. If you want to grow as an artist/human being, you must put yourself out there. Being an artist requires a great deal of courage, stamina, solitude, and perseverance. I need to be in the driver's seat to spend the day my way. You know when you are on the right path when you jump enthusiastically into your work. I still do that, only now I need more sleep!

They say the most important legacy one can leave behind is how you make others feel. My life's work is making people feel great about themselves through my photography and painting. My clients give me such wonderful testimonials that it brings tears to my eyes. I am one happy Artist. Thanks to all of you whom I have touched with my art.

· You mean the world to me.

In 1980 they tried to replace John's pacemaker – he did not make it. He was prepared for this outcome and made certain that I received his works: paintings, sketches, documents, newspaper articles, and photos. His legacy has approximately fifty works of art. John's wish - that I would find appreciative collectors.

To View the John Cabore Collection, please visit our website:

John Cabore collection Art | Florine Duffield Art

https://www.FlorineDuffieldArt.com/john-cabore-collection

Florine Duffield

I have owned photography and fine art studios in NYC, England, Texas & Arizona.

Photography:
I specialize in portraiture, accomplished at retouching those headshots we all need.

Commissioned oil portraits of humans or pets: my favorite, working from excellent photos.

I teach painting workshops at venues including Arizona Artists Guild – painting dogs; how to create beautiful backgrounds.

Made a trip to Barcelona, Spain painting with international artists-exciting!

Last year I jumped into online marketing with Art Storefronts, seven thousand members worldwide. Learning the skills for success through social media.

Member of: Oil Painters of America; Portrait Artists of America; Arizona Artists Guild.

Phone: 623-565-0605
Email: FlorineDuffield@hotmail.com
Website: https://www.FlorineDuffieldArt.com
Website: http://FlorineDuffield.com
Instagram: http://instagram.com/florineduffield
Facebook: https://facebook.com/fduffield

Scan the QR code with your
smartphone or go to:
https://youtu.be/x01U6K0bAqs

The Road to Hana

By Ian Wells Hathcock

*"When you change the way you look at things,
the things you look at change."*

~ Dr. Wayne Dyer

Chapter 12

The Road to Hana

By Ian Wells Hathcock

12.20.2016: After four sun-filled days of playing on the beaches of Maui, my wife (then girlfriend) and I were winding our way through the 600 hairpin turns and 50 bridges in the rainforest of Maui on the "Road to Hana." The rain pounded off the dark black pavement contrasting the dense woods' fluorescent green, providing a perfect canvas for the exquisite masterpiece being painted before us. We marveled at the 200-foot waterfalls that crashed off the rocks as protectors of the seemingly untouched forests, jetting under the roads with an unmerciful force.

We were in awe of the 100-foot palms shaped by nature that leaned into the mountainsides and hung off the cliffs, desperately clinging to life yet somehow dancing freely in the roaring wind. We sat in wonder at the coastal views that rivaled our visions of heaven, and as exquisite as this was, the most beautiful sight of all was not out my windshield but right beside me. Her beauty radiated from the inside out; her kindness flowed into a calming river that poured through my soul, and her ability to love was unlike anything I've ever known.

A breath barely fell between the words in our conversation as we explored the love we shared and delighted in how much happiness our children bring us. She, a mother of three, and I, the father of four, yep, you guessed it, the Brady Bunch in the making; we mulled over how cool God is and was overwhelmed with the joy only he can provide. We were so wrapped up in the moment that we barely saw the car whipping around us as we were heading into a hairpin turn. Quickly, we went from mapping out our future to watching our lives pass before our eyes. I downshifted and guided us to a safe and steady stop. For the first time that day, we sat quietly. Parked halfway off the road, we could hear the idol of the Jeep and the beat of our hearts rapidly pounding. Fear quickly turned to agitation.

Right at that moment, a freight truck came speeding across the bridge that we should have been crossing had it not been for the car forcing us to stop so suddenly. We then realized that the passing car had not almost ended our lives but saved them. Our moods shifted again, this time from agitation to appreciation! We carried on in adventure with grateful hearts and eyes wide open; we were not only seeing the ethereal beauty that surrounded us but all the delicate events that happened to bring us to that place and time. As we unpacked each occurrence, we were blown away, witnessing God's beautiful plan coming together.

In all circumstances, good or bad, we must look beyond what happened *to us* and seek to understand why it happened *for us*. We must begin to see the underlying fabric that knits our lives together to be mindful of seeking the good in all things. We may not always know or understand what each moment is bringing us, but it is important to know that God uses all things for our good. Life is for us, not against us. It can be scary, painful, or even exhilarating, from the loss of a loved one, failed relationships, financial crises, or the trials of our children; nobody gets out of this life without adversity. Suffice it to say we have all experienced pain, some greater than others; I will never compare mine to yours. To get unstuck from pain's vice grip, it is critical to continue to keep moving forward and have an attitude of gratitude in order to experience all the beauty this life has to offer.

At this point, you may be asking, "How did we go from reading about a near miss on the **Road to Hana** to bad things happening to good people?" Well, hang tight. I am getting there. You see, 24 months prior, we were living parallel lives yet without a connection to one another. Daily, we were lost, hurting, and struggling. We could only focus on getting through the next minute of each hour. The thought of a bright future was far too much to even comprehend. Although hurting, we held firm to the knowledge that God provides "Beauty from Ashes" Isiah 61:3. No matter your faith or belief system, I know beyond a doubt as a human race, we are subject to life's mysteries that, are full of joy, pain, beauty, struggle, defeat, victory, and what separates is how we respond. What I can say is with forgiveness, faith, an incredible support system, the love for our children and from our children, it was slowly becoming a success story.

8.20.2015: Then, miraculously, we reconnected; yes, we knew each other before. The beautiful woman sitting next to me on the *Road to Hana* was my younger sister's best friend. I was the antagonizing big brother who taunted them with the "spit thing" that boys do, let it drop as close to her face as possible, then suck it up, pass gas on them when walking by, or, my favorite, pummeling them with dirty football socks. You get the picture; she was like a little sister then. When I was away at college, she grew up too. We later learned our lives intersected many times over the 23-year gap between seeing one another. Surprisingly, we ran across photos of my sister's wedding and had not remembered walking together as Best Man and Maiden of Honor! We were busy in our lives, insignificant to one another, and it simply wasn't our time.

7.27.17: On this blessed day, we were married; our two lives became one, and the nine of us are living out our happily ever after. Albeit with some bumps, bruises, and detours along the way but every day, we choose to see the beauty, embrace the pain, love hard and walk with hearts of gratitude. We have a home full of love and wouldn't change a thing because to change one thing is to change everything. We dance to the rhythm of life and stay in its flow, and we are always amazed at how we continue to grow.

I'll end with this, when looking for a home, we did as expectant homeowners do. We compiled a list of must-haves and deal breakers. I wanted a big grass yard and a pool, she a big kitchen, and a pretty street name. Yes, you read that right, a pretty street name. After looking through hundreds of homes, the sense of defeat started to creep in, but then it happened, and we found The One. It took some work to create the big yard and ideal kitchen, but it was perfect. In negotiating the home, we learned it had been on the market for 500 days, the exact number of days from when we first began courting to the day we got married. Oh, and the name of the street we live on? It's the heavenly "Hana Maui." So, the *Road to Hana* was much more than a day trip; it's where and how we live our lives.

Ian Wells Hathcock

Ian Hathcock is the son of an awesome God, a homeboy with Jesus, husband to his gorgeous wife, and father to seven incredible children.

Ian resides in the beautiful desert of Phoenix, AZ.

He is an outdoor enthusiast who delights in supporting his children's many athletic events. You'll often find him boarding down or hiking up a mountain, in a gym, at a football field, on a bass boat, or leading his team as a Sales Director. Although a collegiate scholarship athlete, Ian's greatest lessons in life were not learned in a classroom but as a student of life who is always learning.

www.Ahavadesign.com

Scan the QR code with your smartphone or go to:
https://youtu.be/FU3sXozx8yo

Mirrors

By Irene Lucas

*"There is something you must always remember.
You are braver than you believe,
stronger than you seem,
and smarter than you think."*

Christopher Robin
Winnie the Pooh

~ A.A. Milne

Chapter 13

Mirrors

By Irene Lucas

Recess! The hot blacktop mushed into soft, pliable goo under my feet while the sun slow-roasted the asphalt, the children, and me. Surveying the playground, I looked for my ten-year-old son Dimitri.

Our children with special needs, now in fourth grade, played alone in their "special ed" area of the K-6 school. I secretly labeled that separate area: solitary confinement.

Innocent of a crime committed, yet still confined, our "non-typical" kids sometimes attempted, each in their unique way, to break through invisible boundaries. Both the boundaries and children shared a similar characteristic: seen but not understood.

Eric, *alone,* stood at the top of the slide, surveying the other children playing with each other. Marilyn, *alone,* scrutinized a foursquare game and inched into line, but somehow it was never her turn. Joaquin, *alone,* lingered near the tether ball line, no one inviting him in. Dimitri, *alone,* stood his observation post by the cyclone fence.

Alas, their typical peers reflected early continuous training in segregation and isolation, inadvertently taught by many of their teachers and an ignorant educational system. Left to their own devices, children are amazing natural supports for one another.

Instead, these typical peers learned to remain separate from non-typical children early on.

My thoughts and heart were troubled with this punitive reality. Typical children learn that their non-typical peers are *less than* and to be avoided, ignored, or dismissed. What happens on playgrounds and in classrooms carries into adulthood, workplaces, and life. What is this isolation and disconnect teaching *all* of our children?

As I watched, overwhelming feelings of love and tenderness for all our special needs children collided with surging, continuing frustration. I felt a familiar sense of failure, and I felt *unworthy*.

As parents, individually and collectively, we tried so hard for so long to transform and integrate this school system, with agonizingly slow results. Our lawyers, plus ACLU attorneys, parent coalitions, letters from members of Congress, and personal and group meetings with school officials resulted in limited success and many unkept promises.

Progress in classrooms and playgrounds crept forward with glacial speed—our children continued to be isolated.

Although we tried our very best, we failed to make the system truly level the playing field, to believe and behave with basic common-sense humanity, to comprehend a clear and basic fact: *separate is not equal.* How hard is that to understand? In segregation, everyone is diminished. In ignorance, everyone loses. Everyone.

Each of you deserves so much better, I thought, watching our fab four and their classmates. We tried our best, but to what end? We attempted to shake the system by the shoulders to make your lives so much more—so much more everything. I felt overwhelmed by another tsunami of love and tenderness. Again, I was haunted by a heavy sense of unworthiness.

As if by a mysterious signal, Eric turned to me from his station on the slide, shot down the ladder, and ran towards me. Marilyn bolted from her foursquare vigil; Joaquin looked my way and abandoned all tetherball hopes. Three 10-year-olds dashed in my direction. Our sentinel Dimitri joined in, taking off towards Mom.

All four came racing towards me, full speed, tennis shoes pounding. Their special ed classmates, seeing them, joined in the charge.

Arms out, mine and theirs. I was literally knocked over by their love, their joy, their devotion, and their trust. We rolled in an unruly mass on the blacktop, laughing, hugging, shouting, reveling in our moment.

Not one of us cared one little bit about the heat or the dirt. Immersed in delight and joy, we ignored the recess bell. Only when the teacher's whistle sounded for the second time did we reluctantly begin to disentangle ourselves.

More than 35 years have passed, and I still remember how it felt to be immersed in so much trust, acceptance, and unconditional love. Our children had *become our guardians* on deep and important spiritual levels. Who in this world is ever this lucky?

Their open hearts, voices, loving eyes, and rolling hugs on the steamy asphalt reminded me: *Worthy I AM. I AM worthy.*

If these children knew we had tried and failed on their behalf so many, many times, they still would have loved all of us unconditionally and not judged any of us. They would have appreciated our efforts and cheered us on. Not for winning or losing—just for being ourselves.

All they could see was Dimitri's mom, always so happy to see them, always loving them, always accepting and admiring them.

How could I know then – there would be many more joyful times and more than a few victories opening up classrooms and playgrounds, sprinkled in among the challenges of transforming an entire educational culture.

I've thought a lot about those moments, that day, our joy, and our children in the community. I've also thought about their open hearts, open minds, and accepting souls, and about those times and all the times which followed.

What I've thought about most is the joy and the lesson I was so privileged to learn – these children, who could only see love and courage and worthiness and devotion in me, wanted me to see that in myself.

Within the careening tangle of assorted blue jeans, T-shirts, and little tennis shoes, they were asking me to love myself as much as they loved me.

Our children, I think, are messengers. Aware on so many levels, each child has an abundance of wisdom to offer – if we can just roto rooter the social static out of our ears to listen, peel open our eyes to see, and pry open our minds to learn.

By trying to get us to see them for who *they truly are,* our children are actually offering us a reflection of who *we truly are.* We are being given the opportunity to recognize our own authenticity, worthiness, Divinity, and ability to love unconditionally.

Our children are speaking to us straight from the heart, trying every possible way they can. *Let's listen.*

Irene Lucas

Irene Lucas is a passionate author, advocate for humanity, especially people with special needs, educational video producer, wife, mother, caregiver, yiayia (Greek for grandmother), and perfect channel of Divine Light.

She is the author of *Thirty Miracles in Thirty Days* and has presented *Sacred Circle, offering* direct communication with angels and holy masters.

Irene is also a writer/producer of several nationally recognized educational videos for people with special needs, including: *Safe and Strong: Safety Training for People with Developmental Disabilities.*

Growing up on the beach in Southern California, Irene is now living brightly on Colorado's Front Range.

Email: ireneslucas@gmail.com
Website: www.irenelucas.com
Facebook: The Universe is Listening

Scan the QR code with your smartphone or go to:
https://youtu.be/Myew4y2gA0g

The White Rose Validation

By Jamie Clark

"Love is a Universal Constant."

~ Jamie Clark

Chapter 14

The White Rose Validation

By Jamie Clark

As I was sitting on my living room couch one morning feeling frustrated, hungry, and broke, I looked at my food shelf and saw that I had only one can of string beans left to eat! I was so tired of being hungry again, and I felt so limited in my life experience. There were many times as a child that I had missed meals before, so this was not something I was unaccustomed to, but I no longer wanted to live this way. I had survived a rough number of years in my youth dealing with a dick-head stepfather with consistent physical abuse, which just added intensity of not wanting to "just" survive life. At nineteen years old, I was already reading and learning about the ability to ask for something from the Universe. However, I was also conscious of giving gratitude as if I had already received it and seeing and feeling as if it was already here, in the present moment.

Brimming with anger that I wasn't living up to my potential, I said to myself and the Universe, "If I have to be poverty-stricken to be spiritual, then I don't need to be spiritual." I felt that If I were working with an "Unconditional, Unlimited God," I should be able to have enough abundance of money, success, happiness, and fulfillment for myself and that there would be enough for everyone on the planet to enjoy. I said to the Universe, "My life is changing, one way or another, by the end of tonight! I accept, see, and feel a single white rose on the edge of this coffee table by the time I get home, and I am not saying a word to anyone beforehand about my validation." I wanted to see if this concept of abundance and creation would play out and how it would manifest. I knew deep in my heart that if this spiritual concept was not validated that I was going to take my own life. This was the deepest and darkest despair that I had ever felt. The turmoil of these constant feelings was shaking my own core, and my faith and trust in the Universe were now put to the ultimate test.

From all the years of bodybuilding, I looked great, but I did not date. I was too ashamed to ask anyone on a date because I had limited resources and was so embarrassed not to live a life I knew I could. So, I got on my ten-speed bike, the only transportation I had, and the only thing I took with me was the acceptance of that white rose on my coffee table when I returned home after work.

I rode twenty miles that day, going to the gym and then to work. I worked as a bartender serving drinks, and that evening I was stationed at the front bar with my eyes on the door when a friend of mine, that I had not seen in months, walked in the door. As she sipped her glass of Rosé wine, she said, "I saw your bike chained up in the back as I was driving by, and I wanted to come in and have a drink with you and catch up." At that very moment, she reached behind her back and brought forward a single white rose from behind her back. She said, "I just wanted to bring you this!" My breath was caught in my chest as my soul soared with freedom! I had not seen her in months! Out of all of the nights, all the kinds of flowers, amounts, and colors she could have chosen, she brought that one single white rose of validation that saved my life, and she didn't even know what she was doing. She was just being her beautiful, effortless, positive self, and she played a major part in saving my life through co-creation rather than manipulating the Universe.

This validation did not shift everything in my reality instantly. Of course, I rode my booty home at 3:00 am in the morning. When

I arrived home, I sat on the couch I had been sitting on earlier and placed my life-saving validation on the coffee table, right where I saw, accepted, and felt it that morning. My life was going to continue, and my faith had been restored. I was now completely open to allowing the Universe to place the people, circumstances, and experiences that would bring me more of what I wanted. I said, "Thank you" to the Universe for manifesting the White Rose. "If I can manifest a rose with you, then I would love to get a car to drive around."

Three weeks later, I bought a Grand Torino. It was used, but it was freedom! I said, "I would love to have a new job and more fun." Three weeks later, I got a new job at Marriott Camelback Inn resort, where I flourished in a hospitality career for seventeen years. Later did, I learn that this was a training ground to be able to communicate with versatility and to be able to talk with anybody and everybody from all social classes. I use this skillset today for my job as a Psychic Medium, TV, radio, podcasting, and public presentations. It prepared me for the direction of my new spiritual life. I was in a frame of mind of openness to life and the experiences being brought to me. I began to use more tools and techniques of manifesting, and one of them is this.

For the next ten days, I would love for you to do two things each day, for ten days.

1) Write down ten things in your life that you are thankful for. Each day, make them all unique so you will have hundred gratitude statements. It can be as easy as, "Thank you for my home. Thank you for the sun that shines on this planet". If the only prayer you pray is "Thank You," that is enough. You will attract more things to be thankful for!

2) Write down ten unique "I AM" statements. Make them all unique and keep it simple. The two most powerful words of creation are "I AM." I AM Happy. I AM Loved. I AM successful and so many more that I AM. Be open to your life

experiences in reaction to your statements and watch how more positive and productive experiences happen and the new people you may attract in a positive and loving way.

Open to receiving life, people, and the experiences and follow the motto, "Live each day as if it is the first day of the rest of my life, rather than the old way of living as if it is my last day."

It is incredibly good to find yourself within life, and it is great to find that life within you and live!

Jamie Clark

Jamie Clark is an Evidential Psychic Medium. With a lifetime of working with his natural gifts, Jamie offers powerful and accurate validations of the spiritual dimensions around us.

As a Metaphysical Teacher, Jamie shares how to integrate the natural psychic senses using the empowerment of spiritual wisdom to help create a more fulfilling life of love, happiness, and success.

Jamie is the Host of the podcast, Psychic Evolution and Author of the "Psychic Evolution Training Cards," "Jamie-isms; Philosophies and Isms of a Psychic Medium," and the children's book series, "The Adventures of Roko and Tookee, The Kids from Mars."

Website: www.jamieclark.net
Psychic Evolution Podcast: www.psychicevolution.net
Facebook: www.facebook.com/jamiepsychic
Instagram: www.instagram.com/jamie5652
Phone: 623-986-6789
Email: insight@jamieclark.net

Scan the QR code with your smartphone or go to:
https://youtu.be/tQiPScUDzP8

When Energies Collide

By Joan Smith

*"I fell in love
with the way you touched me
without using your hands."*

~ Unknown

Chapter 15

When Energies Collide

By Joan Smith

My Dearest Beloved Rick,

I so cherished the twenty-five beautiful years we spent together in this lifetime. You always said you would love me FOREVER AND A DAY – forever on earth and a day in heaven. You told me that you would die a happy man if you died today. You know you were always concerned about my bucket list and what I wanted to do or accomplish. I told you that I had experienced more than I could have ever dreamed. Cards, flowers, and trips. You never forgot a birthday or a holiday, whether with me or with family. You know that everyone loved you and could tell we were so much in love. Every day, when I was working, you would make it a point to kiss me. You also had such a presence in public. Remember when people thought you were Fabio, Richard Branson, or Ron White?

Rick, I think about the magic moment when our love story began. Just to think it all started at my friend Amy's wedding reception. We were perfect strangers, and from a distance, we caught a glimpse of each other. Then it happened in a split second: OUR ENERGIES COLLIDED!

I had never felt anything like it, a serendipitous encounter that had my heart pounding uncontrollably, which lasted all but sixty seconds. Suddenly, I caught a flash of your wife and kids, and my fantasy of you being my soul mate was obliterated. As quickly as that feeling shot through my being, clearly, the circumstances were right, but the timing was definitely all wrong.

My idea of love before meeting you was one-dimensional, one superficial mistake after another.

Then eight years later-

It wasn't until I was 34 and read a book on soulmates that I started the wheels of change. So, I wrote a letter to the infinite universe stating very specifically what kind of partner I wanted in my life – my soulmate, my white knight to come and sweep me away. I needed the one love that fairy tales are made of.

Everything is in divine timing, like my client Bonnie who came into my salon and gave me a book entitled "*The Western Guide to Feng Shui*" by Terah Kathryn Collins. This book was a game-changer in my life. It was all about moving energy or chi, being aware of the yin and yang in my life (masculine and feminine cycles) and making sure all elements were in balance.

I immediately started focusing on the love corner of my home's layout because that area obviously needed a lot of help. Well, what the hell, every corner of my house needed a makeover! So, this is how the magic started. I began in the far right-hand corner of my bedroom, setting up an ode to love. I created a special area with the following items:

- a book of love poetry
- a glass heart of pink and white
- a pair of red candles
- and the love letter to the infinite universe for my soulmate

I could feel you coming, Rick!

Three weeks later–

It was a Thursday evening when I went out to one of my favorite local bars called The Jolly Cork. I was standing at the corner of the bar to get a cocktail and scanned the bar. That's when OUR ENERGIES COLLIDED!

I had to meet you because I felt like I knew you. Then, I did something stupid. I went out on the dance floor with a young guy, came back, and you were walking out the back door.

I truly wanted to throw that moment in reverse. I missed my chance to meet you! So, for the next three weeks, I was on a mission. I returned to The Jolly Cork every Thursday night to find you, Rick. I was driven by the electricity I felt! Then one evening, my friend Linda had just returned from El Paso, so I asked her if she wanted to go out for a drink. I told Linda about this guy that I was searching for, so inside the bar we went. I walked around looking for you. Then, I turned around, and there you were, talking to Linda! I pulled her aside and told her that THAT was the man I had been talking about! She laughed and said, *"Joan, I met Smitty when I was in El Paso. He was working with my husband, and his name is Rick Smith."*

The Introduction

I couldn't believe it! Once again, I felt a very energetic force field between us. You asked me to dance to a song called *"Wonderful Tonight."* The intensity was mind-blowing, with my heart pounding once again out of control. As we melted into each other, OUR ENERGIES COLLIDED!

I felt I had known you before, but where?

Rick, your eyes were looking into my soul from lifetimes ago. You asked me what I wanted, and I responded, *"The Fairy Tale."* You said, "I'll give you the Fairy Tale. Our lot in life is to make people fall in love again." What guy would say this without hesitation unless he was feeling the intoxicating spiritual connection that we had for one another? Then you sang *"Wonderful Tonight"* to me. Twenty-five years later, you were still playing the drums and singing that song for me.

I asked you, *"Why did you walk out of The Jolly Cork that night?"* You replied, *"Because I felt you were out of my league."*

The following week, my friend Amy came into the salon. I was talking to her about this guy I met named "Smitty," Rick Smith, and that he worked at Letterkenny Army Depot. Amy replied, "Joan, that's Rodney's best friend! He was at our wedding reception."

Rick, you were THE ONE, my soulmate, the one I was destined to spend the rest of my life with.

Three years later~

September 17, you took my hand in marriage at the Pennsylvania Renaissance Fair. It was a heavenly union, binding our souls together for another lifetime.

> *"Welcome to the Fairy Tale,*
> *Where Love is an Altered State of Mind."*

~Lord Richard and Lady Joan~

Little did I know that on November 22, 2021, our love would continue, but in the spiritual realm, in a TRULY ALTERED STATE OF MIND.

My Dearest Beloved Rick, your very last words to me were, "I LOVE YOU FOREVER AND A DAY."

My love for you lives on, too.

Eternally Yours,

Joan

Joan Smith

Who Am I?
"Owner of my desires"

What constitutes happiness?

Is it money?

OR

Is it truly manifesting my life's passionate desires, fulfilling my Creative Spirit, being a conduit of Love, Light, and Frequency, bringing beauty from the "Inside Out," making "Elemental Changes" in life's vortexes?

YES, THAT's who I am – Joan Smith.

CONTACT INFORMATION:

FB Inside Out
FB Hot Java
FB ~Elemental Changes~
hotjava1@yahoo.com

Scan the QR code with your smartphone or go to:
https://youtu.be/P_UYXRqqTrg

Angels Fly Forever
Surviving Grief

By Karen Malta

*"For he shall give his angels charge over thee,
to keep thee in all thy ways."*

~ Psalms 91:11

Chapter 16

Angels Fly Forever Surviving Grief

By Karen Malta

I've communicated with angels my entire life, and they have saved my life on more than one occasion. Angels are real. Some are here on Earth, while others are in Heaven. The depth of connecting with angels has never been more intense than since my beloved husband passed away from COVID-19 on January 27, 2021.

My sincere desire is to share a bit of my heart about how I communicate with angels and how they communicate, guide, and comfort us. This writing is a tribute to my Sicilian, Marine cowboy and my adopted brother, Greg Zehring, who truly are my Angels that will fly forever in my heart.

Before I could fully grieve losing my Mom's passing, I lost four other family members, my 2 fur babies "Angel" and "Latte" and then my John. The grief was nearly unbearable and threw me into a severe depression. I suffered from frequent anxiety attacks and insomnia. I was numb and paralyzed with grief. At times I felt I could barely breathe. Life isn't the same after losing someone dear to you. It is no wonder many struggle for decades. Earthly and Heavenly Angels have helped me gain my new life after significant grief.

During my darkest hours, I prayed I would stop breathing. I didn't want to live another minute without my John. What was my purpose? Why did I need to keep living? With no biological children and weak family connections, I felt I didn't matter. I felt so alone. I felt that nobody cared nor would miss me if I was gone. The only ones that seemed to need me were my furry Earth angels, my precious fur babies, "Buttons," and "Sprinkles." They are truly my furry Earth Angels and comfort companions.

Animals are so instinctively intuitive and are Earth Angels, albeit be it furry ones. "Buttons" was John's comfort dog and proudly escorted him to his cancer infusion treatments at the Veteran's hospital. She rode in the basket of his scooter and then laid patiently on his lap while he received treatments. She was quite the hit with the medical staff and the veterans at the hospital. She was able to lay next to John as he transitioned to Heaven, where he was reunited with his family and friends.

My beloved John believed in angels. He recognized that angels literally brought us together.

It began several years before we met when I began an angel doll-making project. It started while I was working for the Arizona Supreme Court. A co-worker had a child, Jacob, who was critically ill. He was being treated at the Phoenix Children's Hospital in Phoenix, Arizona. Despite efforts by some of the best pediatric physicians in the United States, Jacob's condition was not improving. My heart ached for his Mom and my co-worker, Kerri. I wanted to do something for her. I wanted to let her know how much I cared, so one day I decided to use my passion for creative crafts and design something for her.

A girlfriend showed me how to make a rag doll, so I used that as the foundation to design my first angel doll. I made a smaller version of the doll, added wired ribbon for wings, used a glittered pipe cleaner for a halo, and used a piece of ribbon attached to the top of the doll's head for a hanger. The first angel's name was "Faith."

Kerri was touched by my little token of love and compassion, and she displayed it in little Jacob's incubator at the neonatal intensive care unit (NICU). When she saw the name "Faith," she wept. She told me that the doctors had just reported to her that they had done all they could for little Jacob and that they needed to pray and have "Faith."

Sadly, Jacob transitioned from an angel on Earth to an angel in heaven. Kerri said she clung to "Faith" as she left the hospital. To help with her grief, she asked me to show her how I made "Faith." She wanted to make angel dolls like "Faith" for other parents like her who had critically ill children at Phoenix Children's Hospital. Thus, the journey of making angel dolls began. Friends and neighbors learned of my angel project and eagerly wanted to participate. One of my angel makers was Rose Mariel. We frequently communicated by phone and email. She sent an adorable angel email to me. John received one of her emails, and I received his response. Not recognizing his name, I called Rose Marie, and she let me know John was her "cowboy" cousin from California. I replied to his email and soon spoke to him by phone. Our relationship blossomed from there, and we always gave credit to angels for bringing us together.

To date, I have personally made and delivered over 3,500 angel dolls around the world. Nearly 1,000 additional angels have been made at what I call "angel gratitude gatherings," where I demonstrate and show others how to make the dolls. The project's vision is to serve without strings and make angel dolls with unconditional love for unknown recipients who may be dealing with challenges. It's a "pay it forward" type of project.

I can't begin to tell of the many times I've been prompted to make angel dolls with specific colors of fabric and ribbons, specific hair colors, and then prompted to give them specific names. While making an angel doll, I often receive promptings where I intuitively know the proper colors to use for ribbons, fabric, and hair color. It is not uncommon for me to feel the presence of my Grandma Daniels and actually smell her cologne. Ironically, her favorite cologne was "Heaven Scent" by Avon.

As Oprah would say, "Here's what I know for sure" we ALL have angels watching over us, AND we all can receive comfort, guidance, and promptings from them. No matter your beliefs, please know you are not alone. You are worthy of receiving love from heavenly messengers. Here's the secret… YOU MUST ASK! That's right. Angels will respond when requested. They will hear you whether you pray, meditate, or shout out your request.

Whether you believe in God or a higher power or not, I promise you that you matter. You are not alone; you have a purpose and are necessary and needed. Through giving and serving others, I have been blessed beyond measure. I invite you to connect with me by emailing me at TheCariningConnector@gmail.com because connections matter. May you see and recognize the angels among us both here on Earth and our Heavenly Angels. We truly are spiritual beings having a human experience.

I'm a Christian and believe, as my adoptive brother, Greg Zehring, says, "When God can't wait one more day without us, He takes us home." And for me, I know that when our loved ones pass, they become our newest heavenly angels. They will never leave us, and we will simply communicate with them in another, deeper way. Angels truly fly forever and are with us always!

May you always remember that you have angels watching over you, and there is a multitude of Earth Angels whom you will encounter. Be present. Be blessed. ASK to recognize them and receive their guidance and comfort because angels really do fly forever!

Karen Malta

Karen is an Arizona native and is known worldwide as "*The Caring Connector.*" She is a sought-after expert in showing people how to live purposeful lives and manifest joy and wealth by making "*Connections that Matter.*"

Karen is a TV Spokesperson, International Speaker, Best-Selling Author, and Global Entrepreneur. She has appeared on ABC, CBS, and FOX news as an advocate against domestic violence and to raise thousands of dollars for veterans, "Make-A-Wish," and Phoenix Children's Hospital.

Karen served as a Facilitator for *The World Academy for the Future of Women* and co-presented with United Nations Leaders at the 9th Annual Women's Symposium at the Sias International Campus in Xinzheng, China.

Email: TheCaringConnector@gmail.com
Web: www.TheCaringConnector.com
Facebook: https://www.facebook.com/TheCaringConnector

Scan the QR code with your smartphone or go to:
https://youtu.be/DTqj8ssOsjw

Our Mind Affects Our Body

By Kirk Fowler

*"Be nice to everyone.
If they don't appreciate it, be nice anyway."*

~ Mother Teresa

Chapter 17

Our Mind Affects Our Body

By Kirk Fowler

I am grateful to be a part of this inspirational new book, *Golden Wisdom of Love Legends & Legacies*. One never knows what struggles or blessings life will bring, and how one looks at life has a dramatic influence on our health, happiness, and the ability to be a positive influence on others.

Anyone that works in narcotics enforcement spends little time in Sunday School. Narcotic traffickers are filled with self-love, a never-ending desire for more money, cars, houses, etc. To be successful (outside some kid selling joints), they have to use violence against anyone they perceive to be a business threat or anyone who tries to cheat them. If they do not act in this manner, they will soon be out of business.

This is true in the United States (thankfully, not yet as bad) as in many other countries. **PLATA O PLOMO!** This translates as silver or lead. Lead means being shot to death. Silver means to accept bribes. They give government figures the choice. **SICARIO** is what they call a murderer for hire. I have personally been around (sometimes arrested) these individuals. If you look into their eyes, you see no sign of life. Drug lords tempt young men by bribing them with women, firearms, lots of money, and a certain status within their organization. When Cartels become violent, there is no concern for innocent bystanders.

One thing that is essential to understand if you are living in a foreign country, do not expect it to be the same as your country of birth.

EXAMPLE: I was transferred from the Mexican border to the Canadian border while in the Border Patrol. On my first day off, I traveled to Vancouver, BC. I went into a bar, and there were no women inside. I go to a second bar with the same results. I go to a third bar with the same results. I was wondering if women in Vancouver don't drink. I asked the bartender, "Where are the women?" He became angry and sarcastic as he thought I was asking for a prostitute in his fine establishment.

I was embarrassed and returned to Blaine, Washington (my duty station). When I told my friends what happened, they began to laugh and explained to me about the nightlife in Vancouver. At that time, they had a men's side and a women's side in their bars. If you were a man by yourself, you could only drink on the man's side. If you were a woman (or a man with a woman), you could only drink on the women's side. I was told that this came about because, in earlier years, miners and timber men would come to town on weekends, and there were many fights. This law no longer exists.

Mother Teresa said, *"Be nice to everyone. If they don't appreciate it, be nice anyway."*

While stationed in New York City, we arrested a group of traffickers from a South American Country. One of those we arrested had a legitimate humanitarian problem, and one of our Agents took care of this. Years later, this Agent was working undercover in South America. He was with a group of heavily armed traffickers at a jungle airport when he saw the individual he had arrested and later helped in a kind way. Hoping not to be recognized, he walked to the edge of the airport and pretended to be looking out over the jungle. This trafficker walked up behind him and said, "I know who you are, but once you did something kind for me, so I will not say anything, but if I ever see you again, I will kill you myself." It is a good idea to listen and follow the advice of Mother Teresa!

I was raised to respect women. If entering a building, hold the door open; if on a crowded bus and a lady enters, give her your seat. Watch your language and be helpful if there is a need.

It is of vital importance to understand how our mind affects our body. There is a method we can use to verify this for ourselves.

FIRST: Your partner stands to your side and holds your shoulder (holds, not pushes). Walk forward while thinking of someone or something you strongly dislike.

NEXT: Repeat the above test while thinking of someone or something that brings pleasure to your life. The difference is amazing.

ANOTHER TEST: We have a strong tendency to push down negative feelings, which means they will be sort of like a yoyo meaning they will keep pushing up, and we will keep pushing them down. Repeat the above test and walk forward while (mentally) pushing any negative thoughts or feelings down.

NEXT: When we have a negative feeling, be it anger, sorrow, or anything else, mentally open up your chest wide (by wide, I mean like the doors to an airplane hanger) and let the emotions go free. Again, it is incredible to see the difference. When we release negative thoughts or feelings, we open up our body in such a way that natural energy flows throughout our physical body. Any negative thoughts or feelings blocks the flow of our natural energy.

SIMPLE SELF-DEFENSE: Suppose a strong man walks up behind a woman and grabs her shoulders in a bear hug. The tendency is to struggle to get free. Good luck with this one.

INSTEAD: Move your hips to the side and strike him in the groin as hard as you can. If you move your hips to the left side, then use your right hand. When practicing with a partner, do this slowly to avoid injuring each other,

I have been blessed with so many incredible teachers throughout my life that I want to share their kindness and wisdom with everyone I can.

Kirk Fowler

U.S. Navy, Border Patrol, INS Investigations, DEA, Private Investigator. Ki Society Martial Arts over Fifty Years. Grateful father of two kind and caring daughters and one son, I am amazed and delighted by the love, and peace women bring to the world.

Out of gratitude, I wrote the book:
21 Women Who Changed The World
https://amzn.to/3RCFvYw

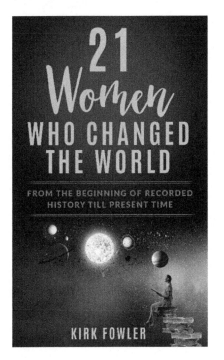

Scan the QR code with your smartphone or go to:
https://youtu.be/sJ9ZlcfyYAA

For the Love of Shawn

By Kirsten Elisabeth Jackson-Hathcock

"White. A blank page or canvas. So many possibilities."

~ Stephen Sondheim (1930 – 2021)
Shawn's favorite quote

Chapter 18

For the Love of Shawn

By Kirsten Elisabeth Jackson-Hathcock

Shawn loved people, was full of hope, reconciliation, and reconnection. His hugs, smile, and wonder just radiated passion. He was beautiful, full of contradictions and taught us a final deafening lesson beyond time, friendship, and the vitality of community. He asks us to forgive, celebrate life, be courageous every day and stay open to the adventures that arise.

My son, Shawn Lewis Hathcock, August 6, 1991, ～ October 7, 2017, is forever the best experience of my life. His tragic death from mental health challenges by way of suicide at age 26 was crushing. That's an understatement. On January 27, 2020, I was gifted an incredibly healing session with Bonnie, an evidentiary medium.

The following is a partial transcript of that session and provides proof of the truth that I believe, "Love Transcends the Veil." The italics represent Bonnie's statements.

* * * ◆ ◆ ◆ * * *

"STOP IT!" Shawn says you are repeating scenes in your head. He says there wasn't anything you could have done to prevent what happened; it was fruitless to talk to him. You kept saying to others, "Shawn needs help." You didn't know what to do as he was so far out there, you felt powerless. He was in total

depression; plus the prescribed meds confused him even more. In his last days, he wasn't making any sense. Coupled with his anger, you questioned exactly when he had his psychotic break. You have reverse-engineered it going back to his childhood, then into his teens. He is so very sorry for the stress and heartache he caused. However, he was living in a completely different reality, bewildered and rambling. He was in his own mental prison enslaved by confusion and emotion. You knew he wasn't on solid ground. You longed for him to be rooted in some sort of reality, but he was floating away from this world. In his memory, please plant a tree for him.

Kirsten responded that she's planning to do it this spring on her grandparent's White Mountain Arizona property. Shawn loves that plan.

Shawn says he knew he wouldn't be on earth long as he was never meant for this world. He was a poetic soul, brilliant composer, musically talented, and a writer who saw the world from a sentimental place, so very differently than others. He was far ahead of his time; action-oriented, visionary, vibrationally intense, bold, and purpose-driven. You often thought, "How did I get a kid like this?" Well, his beautiful ways were just how your precious son Shawn was uniquely created. Even though he was all over the place with inspiring projects, you did your absolute best to help him be more single-minded. You are linear, pragmatic, and efficient. You would caution him that he had to focus; however, without a care, he would say, "Mom, don't worry. I'll figure it out." You did so much for him, and he is forever thankful. He asks for you to always remember him as that sweet little kid, like the photo of him on your wall.

Bonnie and Shawn then shared how we never get over grief, we simply learn to take it with us. There's always a hole in our hearts.

However, as you begin to recall him in happier times, the heaviness will lighten.

You're still finding his things. Although you haven't gone through many of them, you will, in time. He says simply be discerning. Just keep the things that speak to your heart, especially his important work.

Shawn says that you are an extremely strong person. However, you are a caretaker, nurturer, healer, and fixer, and attract needy people. As a troubleshooter, you keep everything going along as smoothly as possible. You're making excellent strides to come out of the black hole to the other side. Your faith has sustained you. At times, standing on the rock of faith was all you had. Abstractly, you know God is always with and for you.

Kirsten, you are highly creative. People don't know this about you. When you recently painted your home's walls, this expressed a side of your many interests. The fresh color positively changed your atmosphere, and you even felt better. He wants you to think of yourself first. You always think of yourself last.

Shawn is pointing out your stunning blue eyes.

Bonnie asked if they were Shawn's color, too.

Oh, wait a minute, he is showing his piercing blue eyes! He also says he LOVES HIS NAME! You were going to name him something else. Jacob? He is chuckling because in no way was he a Jacob. Shawn is deeply connected to his name, which means love. He celebrates his Irish heritage.

He wants you to know there's no such thing as death. He's still working, creating, and loves it. He says his death was not as it seemed. It was painless like he went to sleep and awoke on the other side. Contrary to what everyone thinks, it was a seamless experience. He is completely healed. Shawn emphasized three times: I AM AT PEACE, I AM AT PEACE, I AM AT PEACE!!! Transition and Transformation are beautiful parts of life.

Kirsten, you are not in a hurry. You know you're getting your footing. You are a magnificently complicated, vigilant, morally upright, and compassionate person. Oh, and you will eventually buy a home.

You will continue to feel more solid and realize your dreams. You love to travel to EXOTIC PLACES and will be doing a great deal of that over your lifetime. On a side note, Shawn says he is continuously laughing about the things you get yourself into. He's showing us his favorite blue plaid shirt, which he wore all the time.

His body just hurt; it was a feeling of general malaise. When he went on a self-imposed starvation diet, which he considered a spiritual quest, it sent him further over the edge. Although he could be a bit of a hypochondriac, he experienced debilitating stomach issues.

Shawn says to tell his Grandmother Gawni to continue writing his book. It will be a major multimedia success. With a 2023 publication, its time is coming and will reveal many hidden realities. Its mission funds his Blank Page Foundation with Kirsten as the successful CEO. She capably manages and grows its global outreach.

Bonnie says this is what you are presently learning.

Things in the world will get much worse before they get better. Until we change the cycle, Shawn says history will wash, rinse, and repeat itself. However, we are creating a pristine future now. He says to stay grounded in truth and not let our hearts be troubled.

Our dear friend Karla, who passed away September 16, 2019, arrives singing a duet with Shawn of the song, "Waterfalls" which directly connects Shawn with his dad, Jason Nathaniel Hathcock, July 31, 1971 ~ December 21, 1997 (also age 26). Bonnie is astounded by Shawn's singing voice and was pleasantly surprised to know Karla also has superb gifts. Karla is dancing, ecstatic to be rid of her "Rent-a-Body." In closing, Shawn sings "Happy Trails to You, Until We Meet Again," an homage to his Big Poppa Jay, who is also in Glory.

Indeed, Love Transcends the Veil.

In Memoriam
Shawn Lewis Hathcock, beloved son and family member, loving friend, talented author, writer and composer.

Kirsten Elisabeth Jackson-Hathcock

Shawn's Bio

By Chris Okawa

Shawn's Friend, Voice Actor, and Cricket Sound Founder
Excerpted from Shawn's Eulogy

Scan the QR code with your
smartphone or go to:
https://bit.ly/3fr9zJi

Shawn was everyone's friend because he loved people. They genuinely fascinated him. He was made entirely of hope, wonder, passion, and questions without end. I knew him on many an occasion to fill an entire house with cookies. Imagine that.

He was an idea man, in love with the first spark of creativity, the beginning of a project where anything was possible.

He was unyieldingly ambitious and had the ability to make you believe you could do anything. He radiated warmth and challenged his fellow artists to do the same. Lift one another up. Spread the warm heart.

Mother

By Lisa Beaucher

"I don't know what they're called, the spaces between the seconds, but I think of you always in those intervals."

~ Salvador Plascencia

Chapter 19

Mother

By Lisa Beaucher

The word mother brings up different feelings for many people all over the world. Some relationships are good; some are not. We know everyone has a mother, and we don't get to pick who we get. Luck of the draw? Maybe.

When it comes to mothers-in-law though, well, here we have a choice.

For many people, dealing with their spouse's mother is challenging at best. It's common to see eyes rolling and sighs of defeat during conversations. I'm sure some feel that there is no pleasing this kinswoman no matter what they do. Yet, for many people out there, this is a daily reality.

For myself, I was blessed, and I could not have hand-picked a better mother-in-law. To be honest, I have been singing my mother-in-law's praises to everyone and anyone who will listen for many years.

I met Barbara when I was just a teenager. I remember fondly sitting down together in the "good living room," talking for hours at a time. My boyfriend would call from the other room, "Can I have my girlfriend back now, Mum." Never in my life had I ever felt like I had been seen or heard by anyone, but Barbara knew how to connect. Through the years and because of Barbara's grace and kindness, I began to be myself, and I could talk to her without feeling judged, bad, or stupid. Before this point, I'd never had any adults I trusted in my life, but my heart knew that I was safe with this kindred spirit.

Barbara was refined, intelligent, and kind. She was raised in East Boston and bordered at a catholic school at a young age. After marrying her husband and having five children, she continued her education and received her Master's degree in Education at Boston College.

When my children started to come along, that's when Barbara shined. She was such a wonderful grandmother, or "Grum," as she was known to all her grandchildren. She had a total of eleven grandchildren and six great-grandchildren. She reveled in them all, and Barbara knew how to make each one feel special and cared about. She would delight in their achievements and could lift their spirits when they were feeling down. She cherished her time with them, and the children always looked forward to seeing their Grum. She had a gift for making each child feel like they were the most special person in her heart.

My mother-in-law was a media specialist in the public school system for 30+ years. After she retired, which lasted about 10 minutes, she went to a private school to teach in the library. She was there for almost another eight years. Barbara had such a love for reading and teaching. She delighted in the children she had in class and passed her love of reading down to her students and grandchildren. When the kids would come over for a visit, they would have long conversations with Grum about what books they were reading, who the author was, and what had been their favorite part. Of course, Barbara knew all the stories and all the authors. She knew all the plot twists and endings but would sit and ask questions as if she had never read the book. The kids would answer in delight, giving their opinions about the story and where they thought the author would take them next. She instilled a love of reading which is such a huge gift for each of them to take through life.

She made it a point to have a special bond with each of her grandchildren. They all had their own unique connection and shared great times with one another. Whether it was having a sleepover, going out to lunch, shopping, or just hanging out with Grum and Papa, their bond grew strong. I know that each grandchild has their own favorite story of their grandmother. Then again, I believe that everyone who knew Barbara had their own unique story of her.

I have a difficult time putting into words how much I loved Barbara and how much she meant to me. I called her Mother. Kind of formal and not really my style, yet it felt so natural to use this reference for her. She was well educated, well-mannered, and well-spoken. She knew what she wanted, and she knew how to go about getting it. Her superpowers were kindness, patience, grace, and intelligence. Her ability to connect with people was impressive.

Along with her loving heart, she had a deep sense of curiosity about others. This is what created her magic. When I was with Mother, it felt like being with my soul sister, my best friend. When Mother was with me, I knew everything would be alright. She had such a way of grounding me when I was upset, laughing with me through all the joys of life, and getting my head pointed in the right direction when I was feeling off track. We never had crosswords with each other; there was no need. We understood each other. She always treated me like I was one of her own. I never felt like an in-law, and she never treated me like one. I was included and valued. She was such a gift in my life, and I will always treasure our relationship.

After twenty-seven years of marriage to her son, we called it quits. With a broken heart, I went to Mother's house. She looked me straight in the eyes and said, "Lisa, this changes nothing. You are my daughter, and I love you." Then she gave me the biggest and most loving hug. Her love for me was unconditional. It's not that she didn't see where I went wrong in my marriage or how many times I tripped and fell in life. I think that Mother just saw my humanness and loved me anyway. That's a tall order for any mother-in-law.

Mother was diagnosed with Alzheimer's and dementia in early 2016. She spent her last few years in her hometown's beautiful, assisted living community. Grandchildren from near and far would come to visit. The facility was filled with wonderful caring people who treated Mother with grace and dignity. They showed her the same kind of gentleness that Barbara always treated everyone else with, which was fitting.

She left us in September of 2021. It was evident how impactful she was to her family and grandchildren. She had such a positive influence on everyone. She was a treasure and a true gift for anyone lucky enough to have known her. Through tears of love, we shared our favorite stories of her. Through hugs, we allowed our hearts to grieve. In our family, Barbara was loved; she was a legend and left her open-hearted legacy to everyone.

Lisa Beaucher

Lisa Beaucher created Gentle Hearts Healing to offer her clients Life Activation healing sessions and MAX Meditation sessions. She added additional healing modalities to help adults who are having difficulty getting through life's challenges. Lisa is a certified Life Activation Practitioner, Soma Sound Therapy Practitioner, Emotional Freedom Technique (EFT) Practitioner, and a Reiki Master Teacher. She opened Empower Art Studios on Etsy as a natural creative with a passion for colors and spirituality. Here she displays and sells her beautiful original fluid art paintings. Many of her paintings are infused with positive intentions and sacred geometry to empower you!

Healing Website: www.gentleheartshealing.net
Email: gentleheartshealing@yahoo.com
Artwork Etsy: https://www.etsy.com/shop/empowerartstudios
Email: empowerartstudios@myyahoo.com
Linktree: https://linktr.ee/lisabea

Scan the QR code with your smartphone or go to:
https://youtu.be/NHzx8YGWNv0

Journey of Self-Love

By Lynn Heins

*"All our dreams can come true if
we have the courage to pursue them."*

~ Walt Disney

Chapter 20

Journey of Self-Love

By Lynn Heins

There I was, looking over the edge of the bridge, surrounded by the vastness of green trees, red rocks, and the magical orange and yellow glow of the sunset bouncing off the mountains. This was the beautiful healing energy of Sedona, yet I struggled to breathe and was overwhelmed with sadness.

It was April 1, 2018, and I was standing on the edge of a precipice. It truly felt like I was approaching the end of the world. I was broken, lost, and unsure of myself. I questioned my very existence. I had learned through life's trials and tribulations that I could hide, and I was really good at it. Hiding provided protection from having the world see me muddling through moments of anxiety, depression, and insecurity. How could I possibly share my struggles with people? Who could I trust, and how could I share this vulnerable side of me? After all, I have a professional image to uphold.

At that moment, a subtle shift occurred. Was it a voice, the wind, a spiritual intervention? What I know with absolute certainty is that I had received a clear message, a knowingness that my spirit had awakened. There was a voice deep within expressing this message. There were no words. "It is time to learn how to love your Self." Thus began my journey to self-love.

On that day, standing on Devil's Bridge in Sedona, Arizona, my life forever changed. I had just experienced and survived one of the craziest, most challenging, and life-altering years of my life. I had gone through the complicated and convoluted healing journey that was uterine cancer, divorced my husband after being together for 28 years, and then experienced a breakup with my first girlfriend. My heartbreak seemed unending. I found myself alone in a new state of being called single, living alone, and self-employed. I had learned to protect myself so well that I completely isolated myself from everyone. And there I was. Just me, alone in the space that I had created and alone with my thoughts. Yet, it was in this sacred space of reflection, in this quiet and uninterrupted space, where I finally realized just how broken, hurt, and lost I was feeling inside.

There were moments of questioning God. I earnestly wanted to understand: "Why am I here?" Life felt hard and unmanageable. My self-talk was unruly, and I was mentally beating myself up, demanding, "How did I get here?" I knew the message I received on the mountain was a powerful one. I needed to act NOW. I knew it was time to find myself, and self-love was my saving grace.

I was free of being in a relationship, with the tendency to allow codependency to creep in, worrying more about others than my own needs. I was now living alone, where quiet nights invited thoughts that sometimes spiraled into negative thinking. Yet it was in those quiet moments when I really had the opportunity to get to know me. I knew I needed self-love and self-compassion, but how would I find them? Then the idea came…how to find self-love. Three days after standing on that bridge in Sedona, I was on my journey of self-love.

I recently completed a personal growth class where we measured our progress over 90 days. We focused on areas to improve and measured the results. I decided to embrace the 90-day model and record my awareness, positive moments in self-reflection, and what I learned each day. I broke it down into four areas of my life: Spiritual Connection, Physical Wellness, Financial Literacy, and Relationship with myself and others. Each day, I captured a picture that reflected my thoughts and recorded my thoughts in a journal. To hold myself accountable, I posted my self-love journey on Instagram, each day sharing my passage toward self-love and being vulnerable and publicly visible on the Internet. Accountability was important because we tend to behave differently when we're observed. I needed to remain true to myself.

My first journal entries read as follows:

- Day 1 of loving myself. Took a meditation class followed by a hike to Devil's Bridge. Fed my soul and challenged my body. This is the beginning of my 90-day journey to know myself and love who I am. I included a picture of me on the hike and my Born Free hat.

- Day 2 self-love challenge. Enjoyed a new healthy meal to feed my body. Cauliflower rice, zucchini, yellow squash, mushrooms, peas, carrots, green onion, egg, and chicken breast, all stir-fried in olive oil. Included a picture of my cooked meal.

- Day 3 self-love challenge. Focused on my self-talk. Spoke and thought kind, supportive, encouraging words towards myself. I asked whether I would speak to a friend, sister, partner, or stranger this same way. If not, I would switch. I believe the key to self-love is how we talk to ourselves, so I am up for this challenge today! I included a picture with the quote, "Be nice to yourself. It's hard to be happy when someone is mean to you all the time" (Christine Arylo quote).

As each day passed, I sat with my coffee or tea, journaled, attached my picture, and shared my lesson. These moments were vital to my healing, learning about me, and understanding my shadow self. As day 90 approached, I felt heartbreak all over again. I had expected that on day 91, I would feel different. I decided I needed to do another 90 days of self-love and then, again, another 90 days. I was committed and consistent, and, as a result, I learned much about myself over the course of a year. I took bigger risks, laughed more often, and made new friends. I started celebrating my accomplishments and fell into my value and worth. I was experiencing life fully for the very first time at age 46!

Self-love isn't just a "thing" I do. It's a lifestyle, a different way of being. I am now equipped with the tools to be calm, grounded, and in the present moment.

I've learned that loving myself isn't just a facial or eating right. Self-love is an appreciation of Self — knowing my value, understanding my worth, and being attentive to my happiness and well-being. It's talking to myself in kind and positive ways. It's honoring my boundaries and knowing I am good enough. It's realizing that others' opinions truly have nothing to do with me. I just keep going until I find my people.

There I was. Embracing my captivating eyes, curly red hair, and voluptuous full figure. Owning my child-like spirit. Learning that I can look at myself in the mirror, shed tears, and still be respectful with my words because "I am lovable and worthy of happiness." Truly inspired by the joy I feel inside, I have discovered my spirit. I've created connection to a higher power, learned to look beyond the stories of events, and claimed responsibility for all my decisions. I've learned how to be free within me.

And so here I am, living a lifestyle of self-love.

Lynn Heins

After her spiritual journey to find self-love, Lynn designed a 28-day journey program called Lifestyle of Self-Love™. To support the program, she became a ThetaHealing® Practitioner and Life Coach.

Lynn has spent the last 22 years serving the community as a financial advisor while continuing her hobby as an aesthetician and permanent makeup artist. To answer the calling to support others on their self-love journey, she recently opened a wellness space inside ConXion with her friend, David.

Lynn enjoys hiking, kayaking, hanging out with friends, and trying new cooking recipes. Born and raised in Arizona, she currently lives in Phoenix.

www.lifestyleofselflove.com
Instagram: Lifestyle_of_selflove
lynn@lifestyleofselflove.com

Scan the QR code with your smartphone or go to:
https://youtu.be/PQN3rWzYA2k

Drawing Down The Moon

By Maggie Clark

"Patience is faith applied."

~ Marion Dennis

Chapter 21

Drawing Down The Moon

By Maggie Clark

The altar was set, and all the necessary items to represent the elements were laid perfectly in divine placements. The statue of Kuan Yin with the power of three dragons was surely a sight for the Goddesses. All I needed to do was accept the initiation, light the candles, and commune with the Ascended Master in meditation.

I eagerly and graciously assumed the role of High Priestess for the ceremony. Connecting to my Higher Self, Jesse had given me the confidence to hold an energetic space for all who would be present that evening. Jesse had been a High Priest/Priestess in the temples of Isis at the time when Jesus Christ was delivering his message to the world. Jesse was also a hermaphrodite and growing up in the temple was customary when you didn't fit the norm. The past life memories from this time period felt more real than the present. Of course, this was my Soul Essence, so it should feel like my memories. However, the clarity of that lifetime - tending to the irises in the garden, writing and transcribing the teachings of the time, and preserving the history and ancient mystery school teachings of the Temple of Isis - these memories were magnificent.

No one had taught me how to do the ceremony, but I read lots of books and created a ceremony myself. I loved the energy of the Goddesses, so they were called in to create the realm between the worlds. It was imperative to be able to blend the world of spirit and matter, the living and the dead, and heaven on earth. The Goddesses anchored in the energy of the divine so that we could all connect and ultimately see ourselves as such. The women gathered because of the calling in their hearts to open and express, to have their voices heard in the darkness of night under the power of a full moon, and to have their cups filled with compassion and connection. We stripped naked because, in my world of ceremony and energy, we didn't need hiding places. We had all made a commitment not to judge each other and to share openly. Looking back, I am sure many women entered with fear of being seen, judged, exposed, and vulnerable. Maybe I had had these feelings at one point too, but that was so long ago, and I was happy that fear no longer determined my decisions to cultivate my freedom in all ceremonies.

As the last candle was lit and the circle was cast, we nestled in between worlds and opened up to each other as women. We shared our stories. We shared our tears. We offered gratitude and thanks for the help from the unseen world. We drew Goddess cards to see our own divinity as an expression of the Goddess. We asked for help from our guides, teachers, and women who were present. Most importantly, we had gathered together.

It was an important phase of creating a sisterhood. One that Jesse knew well, surrounded by women in the temple of Isis. The patriarchy had been going on for thousands of years too long, disempowering the feminine and putting masculine energy in a place of more value. This imbalance needed to end quickly. How were we to bring in the New Age without gathering? How could we re-learn trust with our sisters if we didn't come together once a month in our purest nature?

After sharing magical words that hold weight and reverence in a sacred circle, it was time to draw down the moon. This was the first time I remember feeling the energy of channeling. The energy of the moon and the divine feminine in all her silvery light and glory was now being directed into this circle of women. As a High Priestess, I guided everyone into a visualization of a cone of power as I felt the surge of the moon within me. At first, it felt like a cool wash of energy, and then as this vortex was being directed, we spun the energy counterclockwise to draw down the moon's power into the circle. With hands held, this energy blended within our own energy, and all was shared through our words, our breath, and the current of the moon. My body became awash with her essence and her power. I felt as if I was dunked in a bath of divine water that nourished and purified my being, absorbed through my skin, and anchored into the earth through the grounding of my pelvic floor.

I opened and received the blessings of the moon and the Goddess while holding space for all the women in the circle to do the same. My hands pulsed, and my body slightly shook and swayed in the motion of the moon's light and love. My heart was nourished, knowing that this small ceremony with a handful of women could change the world and the consciousness of humanity. This small group could harness the power of the divine feminine with conscious creations and loving intentions. Every spoken word and ceremonial blessing created a ripple of consciousness for everyone on the planet. The feminine would rise into her rightful inheritance as the balance to the divine masculine. This energy arose within me as I welcomed the spirit of Mama Luna.

I channeled the power of the feminine that day and thousands of days since. I channeled my Soul through Jesse, my Higher Self. I channeled the love and beauty of my sisters and their hopes, dreams, thanks, and wishes. I channeled because it was natural. I channeled because I cared. I channeled because the divine nature is what is natural to channel.

As I find myself in ceremony again, twenty or more years later, the same energy of the divine feminine infuses me to show up for women in all stages of life. What desire drives us to be vulnerable and receptive to power, energy, and the Higher Self? We all want to feel love, inclusion, and connection. We all want to return to our Source, our Soul, and to the divine love of the Universe. And until we can fully embody our essence, we can channel those frequencies and vibrations that we can hold within who we are in this very moment in time.

So, ask yourself, where is your passion and creativity asking to express itself? You can channel the divine feminine creative matrix in any experience, ceremony, piece of art, or writing. Every time you receive inspiration, intuition, guidance, and the heartbeat of the Universe, you have an opportunity to feel the flow and grace of feminine empowerment energy through you. Empowerment is an opening, a receiving, a blessing that is divine and feminine. How will you open and receive life at this moment? And remember, when you gather in a powerful group, much like a boulder thrown in a pond, the rippling waves of consciousness travel far. Women in the circle grow and become stronger, meeting eye to eye with compassion. Above all is love.

Maggie Clark

Maggie Clark is the Co-Host of the Podcast, Psychic Evolution, and the Podcast, The Goddess, The Witch & The Womb. The Author of "365 Days of Tarot: Inspirational Tarot for your daily life," Maggie is a respected Tarotist who has been reading Tarot since 1994. As a Spiritual Coach, she uses her background in Metaphysics, Astrology, and Energy Healing to ignite the flame of higher wisdom in others. Maggie is committed to helping people find a way to blend their spiritual life with their everyday life for empowerment, healing, growth, and the facilitation of connecting to Soul purpose and happiness!

Website: www.maggieclark.net
Psychic Evolution Podcast: www.psychicevolution.net
The Goddess, The Witch & The Womb Podcast:
www.goddesswitchwomb.com
Facebook: https://www.facebook.com/maggiejsj
Instagram: https://www.instagram.com/maggiegoddess
Phone: 928-710-6674
Email: mhnorton9@gmail.com

Scan the QR code with your smartphone or go to:
https://youtu.be/FzuxYCDbM0U

The Final Diagnosis

By Marlene Hoskins

"Life is an adventure; it's not a package tour."

~ Eckhart Tolle

Chapter 22

The Final Diagnosis

By Marlene Hoskins

On February 11, 2010, I came down with the most damaging case of Bell's Palsy the doctors had ever witnessed. My small town in the Arizona mountains didn't have the resources to help me. I was left unable to stay upright, watch television, sew, or drive. Riding in the car had me keeping my eyes closed, and I had to traverse any open space with a cane. Bell's Palsy usually goes away in a few weeks to a month at most. I researched hundreds of books, starting with neuroplasticity and anything I could find on self-healing. This was going to be up to me since there seemed to be no help in the medical community.

That research led to finding solace and a whole new world with blogging. My son helped me set up a blog since I was mostly bedridden and primarily housebound for the first two years. My brain was exhausted all the time trying to figure out where "up" was, and I was constantly searching for more information and a supportive community.

The treatments in California helped my face level out, though it was still paralyzed on one side. Treatments in Oregon helped me to drive a few blocks and eventually drive a few miles if I started early in the day. It seemed to some like a small win, but to me, it was huge. What caused the Bell's Palsy? With every fiber of my being, I believe it was brought on by watching my second marriage of 24 years erode and not being able to remedy it. Prolonged stress can be destructive on many levels.

By 2012, the dissolution of our marriage was complete, and I found an apartment in Oregon where I could walk to most of what I needed and drive the short distance to most appointments with my sister and daughter helping fill in where I couldn't manage. Being exceedingly pragmatic, I looked at the small amount of money I had available and thought long and hard about how to make it last without being a burden to my children later. I looked around for two years for a good solution when a home in a park of 525 manufactured homes became available. It was newer than the rest of them and in a quiet location with no one living behind it. My daughter and I decided it seemed perfect. Inspection agreed but said I would need a new roof soon. I was also told that the park could never be sold. That turned out to be untrue. I bought that double-wide manufactured home in June 2014. This was a huge achievement for this then sixty-six-year-old woman with minimal formal education.

The blog turned out to be the best thing I had ever done. Growing up in the gypsy life of a military family, my manufactured home was address number 35. I had learned to make friends quickly, but not the kind of friends I would share difficult things with. For that, I paid a therapist. I smiled a lot and powered through. My new home had brought new stresses. Most days, it felt like the ground was falling out from under me.

Sometimes you just ignore what's really happening until you get hit on the head with a hammer. My 2017 annual checkup brought that hammer down. It was the same diagnosis my mother got in 2000, and my sister got in 2014. "You have Idiopathic Pulmonary Fibrosis." I was the nonsmoker in my family, so it came as a shock.

When mom got this illness, there was only a two-to-five-year life expectancy. We didn't tell her. Mom lasted one year when they found a tumor under her ribs. Seven days later, she was gone. It left me in a tailspin. My sister was doing well, considering she was on oxygen full-time by the time I was diagnosed.

It was time to take care of business. We immediately found a way to put my daughter on the title to the house so she could sell it if I couldn't get that done in time, *just in case*. I didn't need oxygen for the first three years until I started having trouble walking up hills, and I walked four to five days a week to keep pushing my lung capacity. When I needed oxygen to get up the biggest hill, my daughter moved in with me, *just in case*.

I have journaled for the last thirty years. Writing and blogging would help me document and try to understand the process of dealing with this illness. The blogging community sustained me in ways I can't even begin to describe. I wanted to understand what my mother had gone through and never talked about. My therapist kept me on track to live each day fully until the day I let go of life. I put all my affairs in order, gave my son my car since my daughter did most of the driving anyway, and got my house ready to sell.

Then I made a list of how and what I wanted from the rest of my time. I cried quietly when I was alone for a few minutes, then got on with living. The list for address number 35 included a place where I could have my independence and be affordable that still had a community feel. I wanted walkability or public transportation. Writing things down gave me clarity and focus. Then I left it up to the Universe (God) to provide for my needs in whatever ways and means that took. While my daughter and I toured Germany so she could see where I grew up, everything fell into place.

I'm more than five and a half years into this diagnosis, and though I have to be on oxygen full-time since moving back to the White Mountains of Arizona at 6300 feet elevation, the only place available after my manufactured home sold quickly was three blocks from my son and his wife. This place is attached to the Senior Center, which has a kitchen providing Meals on Wheels, breakfast five days a week if I want it, and a shuttle bus at the corner.

I have everything on my list right at my fingertips, along with many other lovely seniors as new friends. I am finally settled and back to doing some sewing and crafting. My daughter is now free to continue pursuing her own dreams. Writing it down is the key. Ask, and you shall receive.

I've defied the odds. My sister is five years younger and had a double lung transplant two years ago. She is defying the odds as well. My pulmonologist said he didn't like the word terminal. He believes in the emerging field of epigenetics, as do I. I plan to be here much longer since I have so much left to do, make, read, and write. I'll continue to document this journey, unafraid.

Marlene Hoskins

Marlene Hoskins was born and spent her formative years living and moving around Germany, attending 13 different schools by the end of high school.

Marlene is a licensed cosmetologist in two states and a certified color and image consultant.

She now resides in the Arizona White Mountains with 36 moves to three countries and nine states. Marlene has finally graduated from the University of Life with countless books that have educated her along the way. At this stage of her life, she continues writing her blog, quilting, and reading every book she can get her hands on.

MARLENE'S BLOG:
https://insearchofitall.wordpress.com/

Scan the QR code with your smartphone or go to:
https://youtu.be/9DdJyPurRhQ

The Gift of Everlasting Love

By Mary Kay Owen

"Be the change you wish to see in the world."

~ Mahatma Gandhi

Chapter 23

The Gift of Everlasting Love

By Mary Kay Owen

It was a cool autumn day, and we were gathered to celebrate my sister's first holy communion. She looked beautiful in her white dress, lacy veil, white gloves, and white Bible, which was draped with her pale pink rosary. She looked like a stunning young bride full of promise of what was to come. We celebrated this event with most of our relatives living in a small town. The church was packed, but we were missing my grandparents, aunt, uncle, and cousins. Later, as we celebrated Marlene's commitment to Jesus, we received the dreadful call. There had been a horrific accident. A drunk driver had hit their car. My Grandfather and aunt, who was pregnant, both died on impact. My uncle and three cousins were in the hospital for months recovering. Everything changed after that day. There were no more weekly trips to the farm to visit my grandparents and cousins. Before my Grandfather died, we would gather at the big farmhouse on the weekends. There was nothing like my Grandma's fried chicken, potato salad, and decadent brownies. There was always a houseful of cousins to play with and meals in the country kitchen that lasted for hours.

I was seven years old when my Grandfather died in that accident. Even though I had such a short time with him while he was alive, he has always been with me. I have continuously sensed his presence. When I was 26, my father passed away. My biggest regret was that I thought he wouldn't be with me to celebrate the birth of my children. However, when my son was born, and I looked into my son's face, my father was smiling back at me! Years later, I mentioned this to my Mom, and she stated that she also saw his face looking back at her when she looked into my son's eyes for the first time.

Our children were very young when I lost my first husband, Jon. At first, I felt hopeless and sad that we would never again have his love and support. I had already lost my Grandfather and father, and the sadness of losing my children's father was too much to bear. I needed help, so I began to meditate. I meditated every day just to soothe the pain in my heart and relieve physical tension in my body. After I began my daily ritual of meditation, I realized I could really tap into the energy of my deceased loved ones. In fact, when I went into a deep meditation, I could feel their presence. I decided to ask if they would squeeze my hand, and suddenly, their energy began pulsing in my hand!

One day as I was playing golf with my son, I asked Jon in my mind to give us a sign that he was with us. Moments later, a hawk circled over our heads and stayed with us! I felt Jon's presence immediately. Then I hit my ball into the sand trap, and the hawk flew right next to my ball and wouldn't leave. Jon had merged his energy with that hawk to say, "I am always with you."

Right before Jon died, he gave my daughter a cat named Penny. Penny was such a source of comfort for Jena. In my heart, I always felt like Jon merged his energy with Penny's to soothe our daughter. Jena was strong and never gave in to her sadness and emotions. She never cried after her father died. Jena cared for Penny until her last year in college. Penny was surrounded with love from all of Jena's friends. One Easter Sunday, Jena called me in an emotional turmoil. Penny was too sick to carry on, and Jena had to put her down. That day, Jena was able to release all those pent-up tears that she had not cried for years. I never mentioned to her that I felt her dad was always with her when she was snuggling Penny. After Penny was laid to rest, I mentioned this to my son, and he validated my feelings when he stated he felt that, too.

My brother Marvin was one of Jon's classmates. When my brother lost his battle with colon cancer, I received the call that it was time to come home for his funeral. I was a wreck. I was booking our airline tickets, and instead of putting my son's name on the ticket, I mistakenly put Jon's name. When I started to pack my daughter's clothes, I reached into the closet to grab a shirt, and Jon's tie was hanging on the shirt. We got to the funeral, and as I talked with my sister-in-law, she mentioned her sister had a dream that my Jon was waiting to greet Marvin in heaven. All those little signs made sense. Jon was telling me, "I will be here to welcome him."

A few years ago, we lost my stepson, Travis. My husband and I had unimaginable pain in our hearts as we went to be with the rest of our family. As we sat together, the lights started flicking on and off in the room where his two young nieces were sleeping. They woke up and instinctively knew that it was their Uncle "T" playing with them. Travis's favorite place was Hinkey Summit. We decided to hike the summit to spread his ashes. It was a tranquil summer's day. We hiked to the top of the mountain with friends and remembered all the good times. We observed a beautiful hawk flying above our heads and could feel Travis's presence in that hawk. There was not a breath of wind on the summit; it was completely still. When it was time to leave, we shouted, "We love you, Travis!" At that moment, a huge powerful gust of wind lasting for several minutes swarmed all around us. Travis wanted us to know he was there with us.

Recently, I decided to pray the rosary with my morning meditations. I had been incorporating the rosary for only a week when I had an appointment with an evidential medium. As soon as our meeting started, my deceased grandmother showed up. She was holding her rosary and made a little joke that "she was happy that she wasn't struck down by lighting for coming through to greet me." The inside joke was that some religions warn people not ever to see a medium. However, the medium went on to say, "WOW! You have over two dozen spirits here to greet you, and they're all holding their rosaries!"

I have had such beautiful connections with my loved ones since I started to tap into their energy that I felt the need to share this joy. To know that they are still with us, and we can communicate with them softens the physical loss. These connections have healed my heart and soul and have given me the benefit of enjoying their love throughout my life. Their energy is powerful and tangible. It is such a blissful gift, and my heart rejoices. I know they are with me now, and their love is everlasting.

Mary Kay Owen

Mary Kay has experienced great love and loss, which led her on a healing journey of self-discovery in which meditation, Reiki, and breathwork were key components.

Mary Kay then became a certified Reiki Master, a certified meditation teacher, a breathwork facilitator, and an international bestselling author.

Mary Kay enjoys connecting with groups and individuals and is extremely passionate and committed to making a difference. She now offers meditation, Reiki, and intuitive counseling at OMC (Owen Meditation Center) in Scottsdale, Arizona, and Flagstaff, Arizona.

Connect with her to be guided into a practice that can transform your life.

Email: Marykayo2011@gmail.com
Facebook: Mary Kay Owen
Instagram: marykayowen

Scan the QR code with your smartphone or go to:
https://youtu.be/IbMCY-MwVM4

Freddie

by Nicoleta Taylor

Anatole France once said that until one has loved an animal, a part of one's Soul remains unawakened. To paraphrase him, until love has transcended human boundaries, a part of the Soul remains dormant. To love people is human. To love all creation is divine.

~ Nicoleta Taylor

Chapter 24

Freddie

by Nicoleta Taylor

Part I:

Freddie the Legend

I live in Phoenix but was born and raised in communist Romania. Back then, the Western civilization was the hushed far-far away land; every so often, bits and pieces of proof that it genuinely existed would "unofficially" make it into the country. In 1982, when I turned 12, I possessed such evidence.

My brother-in-law was a sailor, and one day he brought home posters with foreign artists. It was November, and he let me pick one for my birthday gift. I looked at all of them; they were so different from anything I knew. I was drawn to the image of a man in a tight, black-and-white harlequin suit on a stage with a band in the background, surrounded by bright lights. The caption wrote Queen, each letter a tale itself. Something was captivating about it; maybe it was the man's pose, radiating confidence at its highest, or his looks. I'd never seen anyone like him. Holding onto that small proof that the Western world existed, I kept that poster on my wall for many years.

In December 1989, the people of Romania violently cut the iron bars of the communist cage that isolated them from the rest of the world and tore the Iron Curtain hiding the West. Queen's music broke through, turning my idea of music upside down and inside out. It was love at first hearing, just like the poster was love at first sight. That love channeled a meeting with Freddie Mercury in a dream, backstage at one of his concerts. He talked to me; his embrace felt real. Our paths finally crossed in that timeless space, and we met in spirit. I still vividly remember it after all these years. When *Bohemian Rhapsody* made it to theaters in November 2018, it felt like my 12th birthday gift was fully delivered 36 years after I got my poster. It took me a while to be able to leave the parking lot after the movie; I just sat in my car and cried on my own for a very long time.

Part II:

Freddie the Stray

Around the same time, a peculiar white dog started to show up now and then at a car shop in Tucson; skinny and dusty, yet not a beggar; abused and abandoned, yet still majestic. His amber eyes, lion-like, looked at people as if studying them. Were there any good people left? Could humans redeem themselves and be trusted again? Did they deserve a second chance? Was anyone worth rescuing? Someone at that car shop was willing to try. He took the dog home one night and then to a shelter, where they discovered he was a white German Shepherd, about three years old. They decided to name him Fruitcake in anticipation of Christmas and tried to find him a family. "Nobody likes Fruitcake," said Nancy, the volunteer from the White German Shepherd Rescue who met him after she watched *Bohemian Rhapsody.* "You will be Freddie Mercury!" she declared, then brought him to Phoenix and posted him on Petfinder.

A few months earlier, we lost Max, our loving labradoodle; my husband adopted him the year before we got married. We still had Minnie, his miniature sister, a sweet Terrier-Chihuahua rescued by our daughter when volunteering at a shelter. As much as my family wanted another dog, I wasn't ready. Christmas was nearing, and my heart whispered that opening our home to a dog in need would be the most meaningful present. A frantic search on Craigslist and rescue websites started. Sticking to a limited budget, we were trying to find a medium-size dog that wouldn't shed, was good with people, and was gentle with Minnie. Nothing matched our wishes. On Christmas Eve, too late to find that kind of Christmas present, I went to Petfinder one last time and removed all filters. The name *Freddie Mercury* appeared, and a white dog with amber lion-like eyes looked straight into my Soul. My heart skipped a beat, and all I could think of was, "That's our boy!"

One of the pictures showed him in the shelter "waiting for his Christmas miracle." That picture turned the tables; it was I who wished him to be our Christmas miracle. Christmas Eve was spent writing a heartfelt adoption application. A couple of weeks later, the answer arrived. We were invited to a meet-and-greet with Freddie, but there was a catch – everyone in our household had to be there, no exceptions. The invitation arrived the day before I had to leave town for a two-week job. There was no guarantee that he wouldn't get adopted by someone else during that time. I shared my concern with Nancy, and she replied, "Yes, it is always possible that Freddie will be adopted in the next two weeks, but I'm a firm believer in 'you always wind up with the dog you're supposed to have.'" Her words held true; several people met him, but no one took him home.

During my trip, I would check the website every day after work to see if Freddie was still there. I would look at his picture, love him more each time, and tell him from 2,400 miles away, "You know you're our boy." I would email Nancy to check if he was doing okay. As soon as I arrived back home, we met him at a local dog daycare. When he walked into the meeting room, a profound emotion overwhelmed me, and all I could do was cry. He circled the entire room with his leonine royal steps, and we brushed our fingers against his silky white coat. He kissed Minnie on her nose, jumped up, put his paws on Nancy's shoulders, and then came and laid at my feet. He sighed; it felt like he recognized us. At that moment, he was perfect to my family and me, and he stole our hearts forever.

Part III:

Freddie's Love Legacy

There are so many reasons to be grateful for the real Freddie Mercury. For fans, it's his extraordinary voice and music; for Queen, it's his genius; for Rami Malek, it's a Golden Globe and a greatly-deserved Oscar. For us, it's Freddie - the loving, intelligent, gentle, loyal, majestic white German Shepherd dog who came into our family and became the champion of our hearts (*We Are the Champions* is playing right now in the background of my mind). For Freddie, the dog, it's restoring his faith in humans. As Nancy put it on the successful adoptions page of her rescue, "Sweet and friendly Freddie Mercury has found his forever band."

I published Terrans, my legacy book, three years after he joined our family. In the *Gratitude* chapter, next to all of the names important to me, I wrote: "Freddie, our white German Shepherd, the non-human love of my life." It is only fitting to wrap this true story up by quoting Freddie. One day he asked me, "Share this, and it might inspire others. Someone else's champion is in a rescue, waiting for forever love in a forever home."

Nicoleta Taylor

Nicoleta Taylor is an American author born in Transylvania, Romania, where her writing skills gained national recognition.

In 2010, she married her American soulmate and moved to Phoenix, Arizona, where she rebuilt her life and started writing again.

On Earth Day 2022, she published her first book "Terrans: To MotherShip Terra's Stewards, with Love," an Amazon bestseller in inspirational poetry. It transcribes the broadcast of a human passenger of MotherShip Terra, our planet, that intriguingly coalesces science fiction with spirituality.

She is also a proud contributor to "Wisdom of the Silver Sisters - Guiding Grace," a #1 Amazon international bestseller.

www.nicoletataylor.com
https://amzn.to/3TEFaFC

Follow the Yellow Brick Road

By Norma-Jean Strickland

L   "Look

    I   Inside

        F   For

           E   Everything."

From NJ's first book,
"BITE-SIZED PRAYERS: Non-Denominational
Morsels to Feed Your Soul"

Chapter 25

Follow the Yellow Brick Road

By Norma-Jean Strickland

When I was growing up, I had my life planned as far ahead as I could think. Nothing would change my mind. I just knew what I would do professionally and then the rest of my life would fall into place.

Well, things didn't go as I had originally planned at all! I have actually traveled a rather circuitous path in my lifetime, both professionally and personally. There have been many moments when I have wondered whether I was just letting life happen to me or if there was any clear direction for the way I was moving.

There are certain recurring themes in my life that lead me to believe my steps have guided me to the place where I am now. I'm not certain I would change anything because I'm grateful for everything I have accomplished and experienced, most of which I could never have predicted. What I might change is how I have (or have not) directed my own life to this point. Isn't that part of the reason for growing up, to become mature and wise and lead others by example so they can learn from your hard-won life lessons?

Perhaps you've heard the expression, "Follow the path of least resistance." That doesn't mean to be lazy or take the easy way out.

What that means to me is to take the path that rings true for you, the path that aligns with what makes you feel alive and full of passion. I confess that I haven't always done that. I've taken jobs just because I needed the money and then wound up being miserably unhappy, not wanting to wake up and face the day because of doing something unfulfilling.

For the most part, I feel like I've paid a high price for expressing my creative freedom and independence, but I would do it all again in a heartbeat! Life is far too short to spend precious time doing something you don't enjoy. Granted, there are aspects to some projects that might be tedious but, in the overall scheme of things, that's just part of getting to the point of completion. Everything occurs in cycles. Just look at nature. Planting seeds, germinating, giving birth, growing, fully blooming, withering, decaying, dying. Repeat.

There's another expression you may have heard that says, "Where intention goes, energy flows." A slight variation is, "Where attention goes, energy flows." There are schools of thought that say, "Change your thinking, change your life." I believe this with my whole heart, even if it has taken me a lifetime to learn it.

Sometimes, the Universe (Source, God, Awareness, whatever word you choose) has a guiding hand in leading you to make specific decisions, whether you're aware of this guidance or not. Often, you don't put all the puzzle pieces together until long "after the fact." Here's just one example from my own life.

I had been living in a one-bedroom apartment in a location that made me miserably unhappy. As the end of my lease approached, I was earnestly looking for another place to live. Although I was only renting, I decided to contact a real estate agent. As it happened, she had a renter who was leaving her lease early and was willing to let me take over the rest of that person's lease. It turned out to be a beautiful home, which is the first house I've ever lived in since graduating from high school and leaving my parents to go to college. Until now, I had always lived in apartments. This new place was a 3-bedroom, 2-full-bath 1,459 sq.ft. house with an attached 2-car garage with both front and back porches and yards.

While I was packing and getting things ready to move, I kept getting this urge to buy a certain oversized chair that was the softest leather I had ever felt. It could easily fit two people and open up to lie flat. I went back to the store at least three times and eventually bought it. The bonus was that it was on sale!

Little did I know that when my father's wife passed away less than a year later, he would come to live with me in this house. Since I used two of my bedrooms as my music room and my office, my father got my master bedroom. I wound up sleeping on that oversized leather chair for over five months until I moved him into an assisted living facility.

And guess who my next-door neighbor was? The owner of two assisted living facilities, both small private residences in gated communities. My neighbor was from Poland, so everything was very quaint, homey, and charming. She later sold it to another Polish couple. My father loved living there and was happier than ever. I am deeply grateful because being a 24/7 caregiver is the hardest thing I have ever done. He wound up living there just three weeks shy of five years before passing away, barely one week after his 95th birthday.

The peace I have from knowing my father was happy and safe – and the fact that I got to have my freedom and independence and actually live my life – is priceless. This time also allowed us to become closer. Although he had progressive dementia, we had countless meaningful conversations. He said things to me that I had waited a lifetime to hear.

SOOOO. . .it would appear that the Universe had a guiding hand in my coming to live in THAT house, next to THAT neighbor, and buying THAT chair! How did the Universe know what was coming ahead? I am so glad that I PAID ATTENTION! I want to learn more about this mystery!

My daily focus is becoming to make conscious choices in every moment. It's not always easy (yet), but it's important enough to make the effort, be aware and be self-disciplined. Practiced enough, it will become as natural and second nature as breathing. Then my life will flow easily from the inside out and I'll be following my own yellow brick road to wonderful new adventures!

Now I'll ask you, the reader, to consider the following question:

Are you following your yellow brick road?

Norma-Jean Strickland

"NJ" is a writer, educator, speaker, classical musician, photographer, colorful character, and curious creature! She has touched the lives of thousands of people in meaningful ways. Her vision is to bring love, joy, and healing to the human heart through story, music, and play!

"NJ" has spent a few years focusing on new and emerging research in the fields of quantum physics, epigenetics, DNA reprogramming, and cymatics. She finds all this combined information utterly fascinating. She possesses an insatiable curiosity about the mysteries of life and hopes to create something that bridges these different fields.

She welcomes opportunities to collaborate.

WEBSITES:
https://njstrickland.wixsite.com/starlightcreativepro
https://www.linkedin.com/in/normajeanstrickland/

Scan the QR code with your smartphone or go to:
https://youtu.be/bfiHiG6fHe0

Conjuring Joy

Patricia Breed

"When you know better, you do better."

~ Maya Angelou

Chapter 26

Conjuring Joy

By Patricia Breed

I excitedly punched in the code for the Airbnb. The description of the airy A-frame boasted a modern yet inviting interior nestled in the woods overlooking the spring-fed lake, and then: POW! An intense chemical-infused floral odor accosted my nasal passages, my skin immediately began to itch & eyes burned. I scanned the space desperately trying to locate the plug-in before a migraine ruined our coveted rest-bit in nature. I quickly realized it was only one of many well-intentioned sensory assailants waiting to welcome us.

More, it was a visceral reminder of why I do what I do!

I genuinely believe the host's intention is for their guests to feel welcome. Even the intense toxic odor was a good yet misguided intention.

As a young professional adhering to a gluten-free, pescatarian diet, avoiding the dirty dozen, and practicing yoga, I invested time, energy, and money in my health & wellbeing and was frustrated by the ROI. So when my acupuncturist asked, "have you considered your environment?" I listened.

A self-confessed clean freak, I obsessively eradicated germs & grime with a mixture of bleach & water in spray bottles placed conveniently every 10-15 feet for ease of use. My loft was a clean, uncluttered &

organized space. I always looked forward to returning home from the frequent & long business trips. On the road, I always had disinfecting wipes on my person. Have you seen the exposes on airplane trays, remotes in hotel rooms, and the steering wheels in rental cars? Gross! My spacious loft was my CLEAN sanctuary. Or was it?

As an artist, I focused on how our relationships & interactions in our environments shaped our identities. Thus, it was logical that our homes and workspaces impacted our health & wellbeing. Yet, what was the trigger?

I fell back on what I learned in art school: be a critical observer, question what you see, seek information, and solve problems through a series of visual experiments.

I honestly cannot recall why I focused on the cleaning products; likely; it was due to their outsized presence in my life.

I quickly learned bleach & commercial cleaning products did not support my health & wellbeing. Bleach is an effective disinfectant, yet it is a respiratory, as well as nasal, throat & skin irritant. It is also the worst choice to clean your cat's litter box. I mention this because I am a proud cat lady that was horrified to learn the ammonia in cat urine & bleach combine to create noxious fumes causing a dangerous environment for humans and cats.

I removed all the spray bottles filled with bleach & water from my home. Within a month, there was a notable improvement. Life continued, and that might have been it, except after 15 years in higher education & not for profit, I resigned effective immediately. Yet, I needed income. I was not eager to begin the job search and not quite sure what I ought to do; my partner shared that the happiest he remembered was when I worked for myself. During the 2008 Great Recession, I briefly operated a green cleaning business, The Clean Witch. I still had the marketing, and until I figured out what was next, it was a readymade option.

Except, I didn't want to use any 'green' cleaners. Through the years, I continued my cleaning product research and learned many dirty secrets. The FDA does not regulate cleaning products or deodorizers. The EPA requires only the active disinfectant and hazardous chemicals at 100 parts per million to be listed. To put that in perspective, one scientific journal describes it as one minute in two years. My intention was for my home to be clean and healthy. I do not see these as competing goals. Almost always, 'green' cleaning products contain fragrances, even if they also contain essential oils. Federal law does not require fragrance ingredients to be listed; it is protected under the Trade Secret Law.

Fragrance can contain solvents, UV stabilizers, preservatives, and dyes. Phthalates, commonly utilized in fragrances to extend their smell, are hormone disrupters and linked to neurological disorders and cancer. For decades, I cleaned my home with humble, non-toxic, biodegradable ingredients found in most household pantries. I have yet to meet anyone that likes the smell of vinegar. Our society likes our homes to smell, as evidenced by the numerous candles, plug-ins, sprays, scented trash ash, and toilet paper rolls. I utilized essential oils for their therapeutic benefits. I began researching oils for their functional benefits.

Awww, life is not linear. It is a collage as I was increasing my knowledge of essential oils, experimenting, and enjoying making eco-friendly cleaning products. Mixing the essential oils reminds me of blending oil paints to get the exact color.

At the same time, the cleaning biz calendar was booked, and I could not shake this feeling it wasn't what I wanted or needed. Then a friend asked if I was familiar with Feng Shui. I recalled it from the eastern art history classes, but that was about it. She suggested I read Terah Kathyrn Collins Guide to Western Feng Shui. The more I read, the more I realized I needed to know more. Enrolling in the Western Feng Shui School in Sedona confirmed it was time for The Clean Witch to transform, to be for the Eco, Health & Chi

Conscious. Everyone/Everything is composed of energy, and energy is connected; energy is forever changing

Our homes are much more than crash pads and storage facilities for all our stuff. We are in a relationship with our homes. You have the power to decide whether to continue a toxic or a healthy relationship? You can align your values & intentions with your home. Our home is the one partner we can change to have our ideal relationship. More, you can determine how and improve your quality of life.

Holistic means encompassing the whole of a thing and not just a part. I don't think we clean our spaces. We cleanse. We remove dust, stagnant energy and intentionally release it. What we clean with matters. I like to say The Clean Witch Cleansing potions were experientially created & tested. It began with brewing potions for my client's homes. I am mindful of & consider the energy of their home, the season, and the elements and decide which oils balance the energy and effectively cleanse their space. Presently, The Clean Witch sells organic cleansing potions brewed with non-toxic, biodegradable ingredients, a proprietary blend of 100% pure essential oils & intention.

More, I am grateful for my clients. They recommended I sell my cleaning potions; also, because of their sharing concerns, like lack of concentration, sinuses, and difficulty sleeping, I developed the spell sprays - aromatherapy for home and wellbeing. I fell back on what I learned in art school be a critical observer, question what you see, seek information, and solve problems through a series of visual experiments.

With our intention of Dwelling in Joy, we offer Decluttering, Organic Cleansing, Feng Shui, and Holistic Living Apothecary.

Patricia Breed

Trish Breed earned a BFA in Studio & Art History from the Kansas City Art Institute, studied at Victorian College of the Arts in Melbourne, AU.

Represented the School of Art Institute of Chicago & the San Francisco Art Institute, before learning to "see with Feng Shui eyes" at the Western School of Feng Shui. In 2017, she began Conjuring Joy for the Eco, Health & Chi Conscious.

Trish@TheCleanWitch.com
www.TheCleanWitch.com

A Legacy of Love, Music and an Organ

By Patricia Holgate Haney

*"What you leave behind is not what is engraved
in stone monuments, but what is woven
into the lives of others."*

~ Pericles

Chapter 27

A Legacy of Love, Music and an Organ

By Patricia Holgate Haney

My Great-Grandmother's home was a tidy, compact house without many of the usual collections of ornamental dust catchers. Visiting when I was young was fun, but it was not a visit full of animated discussions and laughter like we had when visiting Dad's parents,

Occasionally I overheard snippets of personal stories from the adult conversations. My attention was drawn to the tidy parlor containing a pump organ. I had never seen anything like it except in a movie.

My knowledge about the organ was limited, knowing only that pride and sentimental value were attached to it. With wonder, I ran my hands along the top of the organ, feeling the smooth, well-worn wood. Carefully I opened the wooden cover, my hands skipped over the keys, and my imagination ran wild. Who had played the organ?

What did it sound like? Where had the organ come from?

When Great Grandma passed in the 1960s, my Dad inherited the organ. Taking months, he painstakingly refinished it and replaced some of the worn felt near the pedals. It was beautiful. He had tried to honor his inheritance by refinishing it, only to be told by "experts" he probably should not have done so.

The value to me is in the rich history. The organ is intertwined with fearless pioneers, of California and my family legacy. It became a catalyst for Dad's deep dive into genealogy, beginning in earnest once he retired.

He visited genealogy libraries and wrote letters to distant relatives he found. He collected personal recollections, which provided additional clues and branches.

Dad used his dial-up internet service and a dot matrix printer to compile copies of the records he discovered. Not driven by a need to find out which famous person we may be related to, instead wondering how we had arrived here, what transpired during the journey and what their lives were like.

Dad had begun writing a book with no end. His lifelong love of the written word, natural curiosity, and his ability to not take things too seriously are what I will always remember.

He had special three-ring notebooks imprinted with a title that perfectly illustrates his sense of humor. Our family history notebooks are titled *Counts and No Counts.*

The opening line of his introduction reads, "For why is this being writ? Because our understanding of what this weighty book is about is important."

The book contains documentation that Schofield Holgate, my great-great Grandfather, was born in England, and his musical talents were developed there. Arriving in California, he and his family settled in what would later become Norwalk. A handwritten account, along with a published book on the history of Norwalk, gives the following information:

Schofield Holgate (aka "Professor") and his Daughter Julia brought their musical talents to the community far and wide.

"At one time, the Professor and Julia would arrive in their wagon at the Old Dickerson Hop House. Once the crops were sold, and the hop house was empty, it became the center of attention for those who danced."

When the wagon arrived, excited and willing neighbors would carry the organ up the steep stairs to the loft. Schofield played the violin or fiddle, and Julia the organ.

The loft was "so large that two sets of quadrille circles could be danced at once; a typical dance evening was attended by many people who could not dance the round dance, so every other dance was a quadrille. Therefore, there was no whooping or yelling as the radio entertainers would lead one to believe."

All descriptions sound like a period movie. "The women prepared refreshments, and very young children were put to sleep somewhere convenient."

The Professor and Julia began playing around eight o'clock in the evening. At midnight, refreshments were consumed, and the dancing continued until daylight.

Later, the Old Social Hall was built as a dance hall by members of the town band and their leader Schofield, becoming the pride of Norwalk.

One handwritten account closed with "many of those mentioned have gone on the long, long trail, but their works were not in vain, for by such pioneers was the foundation of the great state of California laid" - *Submitted by Helen Brown* for our family records.

My Grandfather loved to dance. He met my Grandmother at one of the many dances held in ballrooms around Los Angeles. My Grams family were "late comers" to California, not arriving until 1912. She brought her love of laughter, music, and dance to California from Missouri. My Grandparents danced until they were separated by death.

My Dad loved music. He especially loved big band music and jazz. Mom loved music and told stories of her upbringing in Iowa; she and her best friend and cousin Jeannie would sit on a hill above the community band shell listening to the music, dreaming of their futures. When she met my Dad, they loved to dance together and did until they could no longer do so.

After Dad and Mom passed, the organ found a new home with me. The organ is a living piece of history. Dad found many stories, but there are more to be discovered.

For me, the organ represents how music touched my family and the part it played in history. I can sit in front of the organ and attempt to play. My great-grandchildren love to try and play it. I've told them the stories of the organ, and they have fun but are respectful of the history and the fact that it is old, older than me!

Dad left us with a legacy of information, and along the way, he shared his skills with others through Paradise Genealogical Society until he was physically unable. He even traced a headstone that had been removed and dumped for decades back to the location it belonged and gave a sense of peace to that family.

I love the personal stories more than the lineage information. I know that you cannot have one without the other, yet by reading the stories, I see traits that indicate where my sense of adventure came from. We even had relatives who were victims of the Connecticut Witch Trials. That could explain a lot of things, I'm sure.

My sister Nancy is continuing Dad's quest for family lineage and is fantastic. I continue to collect and recall personal stories. I believe these are the most valuable legacies we can leave when we are gone.

I don't want to leave my children the burden of going through items they have no interest in or need for. I want them to know the stories about the few pieces I have that I believe have significant history, yet I don't expect them to automatically feel the same. I have looked at different historical museums where, if not wanted, they would welcome the items for the documentation of history.

I am, therefore, leaving this story and my Dad's dedication as a legacy. A written account that can be read at will.

The last paragraph of Dad's introduction *to Counts and No Counts* reads,

> *"Some people like to describe themselves as dedicated. This is something you do to a cornerstone of a building. Some like to leave something when they go. The only trouble here is that someone else must clean it up. Think of what might have occurred if this effort had been directed toward something with a monetary value. How would the four of you divide up two cents? Enjoy."*
> *- William C. Holgate 1926-2006*

Patricia Holgate Haney

Inspired by a love of books passed down by her father, she immersed herself in the written word and dreamed of exploring the world.

With her husband Gary, she continues to explore the world with insatiable curiosity and enthusiasm, reveling in the opportunities to meet new people, share experiences where places from pages come alive.

At home, she enjoys time with her husband and family which includes two sons, three grandchildren and three great grandchildren.

After careers in both the non-profit and for-profit corporations, she focuses on writing and has been published in seven compilation books and is currently working on a solo book.

She volunteers for organizations that are dedicated to helping the underserved and ensuring equality for all Profits for the sale of books on her website are used to provide for the unsheltered.

She lovingly polishes the organ and continues to collect stories of times gone by.

E-mail: seaglass@phtravels.com
Website: www.phtravels.com

Scan the code or go to:
https://youtu.be/P3G6Y8xqFjw

Amazon: https://www.amazon.com/author/patriciaholgatehaney

Death:

A Most Feared Illusion Debunked and Proof of Heaven

By Ron Baron

"Reality is an illusion, albeit a persistent one."

~ Dr. Albert Einstein (1879 – 1955)

$\mathcal{D}eath$:

A Most Feared Illusion Debunked and Proof of Heaven

By Ron Baron

In the winter of 2005, I received my greatest challenge and my greatest gift. Doctors diagnosed me with a rare head and neck cancer, giving me only three to six months to live. Frightened by the idea of cancer and my new life expectancy, I quickly found the appropriate treatment protocol.

The six weeks of radiating my head and neck, concurrent with chemotherapy, was a brutal and inhumane protocol, causing a loss of 60 pounds in six weeks.

To date, radiation aftermath remains one of my greatest life challenges. During the protocol, I received a gift that permanently altered my life – a Near-Death Experience (NDE).

Almost 17 years later, I still remember it in vivid detail. On a cold winter's afternoon, while asleep on a couch, my body lifted up and out of itself and rose to about 13 feet in the air. I looked down and saw myself sleeping. I lay on the couch, with my eyes closed, and saw myself hovering above myself. If that wasn't crazy enough, while I was hovering, I split again into a third me, but that 'me' didn't hover. I was gone in a flash, leaving a light white stream of something I'd now say was energy because it was too light and translucent to be smoke.

The third me went into space; stars were still millions of miles away as I was peacefully floating in awe. What appeared next was extraordinary – a full-length, one-dimensional door. When I floated around behind the door, it had vanished, and then when I floated back around, the door reappeared.

I was curious to see what was inside. With a deep sense of peace and absence of fear, I opened the door and saw the strangest thing – a room that resembled an old library filled with great character. It was unfamiliar to me, and although I can still recall it in great detail, I'll remain focused on the most important part to share with you. The lit fireplace and authentic wood-paneled walls were surrounded by bookshelves filled with books and artifacts.

I poked my head in slightly to get a sense of it and noticed the door in the far-right corner. It soon opened, and no one that was a stranger to me came into the room, all of whom had passed. Mom and dad, aunts, and uncles, and even my beloved dogs, whom I was blessed to have loved, were there – all took their places in the room. Mom sat in the center chair facing me. There was such calm and peace, and everyone had a sense of euphoria and lightness about them. I took the time to look into everyone's eyes, and as I took it all in, I understood what euphoria was like. Looking at mom, I noticed beams of light that began illuminating out from the sides of her body, as well as from the top of her head. Without a word spoken, she told me how wonderful it was to see me and that I was not ready to join them. This amazing vibrational state of euphoria was one that I wished would last forever.

In an instant, I was back in my body. I jumped off the couch and, like childbirth, was gasping to get air into my lungs. A dear friend who was with me in the room thought at that point that I might be dying when, in fact, I had just returned from wherever I went. Without a clue of what had just happened, I told no one.

Happy with retrospection, I realized that on the other side of the doorway through which my family had entered was that place we call heaven. During those moments, my consciousness was so expanded and heightened that I maintained awareness of being in three places at the same time, which to date, remains something beyond words. I learned that the process of transitioning is nothing short of blissful and utterly indescribable.

Unbeknownst to me, this greater consciousness has blessed me with an ability to channel infinite possibilities more easily, which has permanently altered my human experience. I am not the same man I was. It took two to three years of elaborate processing time for me to responsibly assess and interpret what had occurred and what I made it all mean.

It's my privilege to now share the Cliffs Notes version of what the amazing "take home" was.

Spiritual awareness tells us that we are spiritual beings having a human experience. When I expanded out of my mind and body, what was left? It doesn't matter if we call it spirit, soul, individual consciousness, or whatever you choose. I am neither my mind (including personality and identity) nor am I my body. I simply am that I am.

Expanding outside of my mind and the physical body removed my ability to see, hear, or comprehend anything, and yet, how was it possible that I did? Plus, the conversation I had with mom occurred without words. There were infinite possibilities at play, from which my mind was left to interpret. Placing ego aside and understanding how the mind works to process thought energy, my mind needed to make up a story about what had happened to comprehend and relate to it in my human reality. Why did I see loved ones and not some strangers from a different continent speaking in their native language or aliens speaking a language I didn't understand? Although my mom didn't speak, I heard her voice in my head as I remembered her, or did I?

After realizing that the interpretation of the experience of what had occurred was all created in hindsight, I understood that it was the only way for my mind to understand the incomprehensible.

One of my favorite quotes from Dr. Albert Einstein is, "Reality is an illusion, albeit a persistent one." That statement makes so much more sense to me now.

To be inside a human form, I needed to consider what happened during my NDE. My new understanding, like all aspects of reality, is that everything is one big made-up illusion, and, more importantly, I'm the one who makes it up. The proof of heaven was not what I thought I had seen or the messages I had received. It was the fact that I left my body, went somewhere else, had an experience, and then returned to my physical form. This was right under my nose, and I finally caught it. Near-Death Experiences may well overlap in the storytelling, but their interpretations are unique to what each mind chooses to make up, based on each individual's past experiences.

Living life inside of an illusion, where I'm the final author and editor of my autobiographical novel, is all I've got for the moment. Any great hurdles ahead that challenge me will eventually be so far behind me that they will no longer be in view, only remembered. The continual simultaneous transformation of who I am being and who I'm becoming will last throughout my lifetime, allowing every hurdle to have served its purpose.

Ron Baron

I'm a Brooklyn-born and raised Italian version of Enlightening Consciousness who helps minister and transform realities.

Assimilating changes that last a lifetime requires discipline, training, and practice and places me at your service.

I offer a 100% Guarantee, or you get your Old Life Back!

- Bachelor of Science degrees in Biology and Psychology from SUNY Stony Brook University
- Near-Death Experience Graduate, for which there is no degree
- Landmark Education Curriculum Graduate
- Transformational Reality Coach
- Devoted Yogi and Vegetarian
- Bodywork Therapist
- Creator of Quantum Gliding, Baron's Mini-Meditations, and The Freedom Warrior LifeStyle Training
- Entrepreneur and Visionary
- Authentic Urban Cowboy

CONTACT INFORMATION:
https://www.barontransformations.com

Scan the QR code with your smartphone or go to:
https://youtu.be/hnGQDleU4HY

About Journaling:

The Story of a Legend and Her Legacy

By Sandy Rogers

"Twilight's rays of whisper gray filters through my window.
Time has passed and I wondered if I would rest,
For I had wandered through many nights,
which had no sleep at all.
Endless, restless nights have come and gone through the years,
Wearing and tearing, yielding, and building
both the body and the mind."

~ Doreene Clement (1951 – 2007)

About Journaling:

The Story of a Legend and Her Legacy

By Sandy Rogers

I first met Doreene Clement in mid-2000, shortly after she developed, self-published, and launched her book *The 5 Year Journal*. This book, with a hardback, dark green leatherette cover, acid-free pages, and a satin ribbon divider, offered a way to journal just three lines a day for five years on one page. It also had a workbook section to summarize each quarter.

She was one of those people who, when you meet them, you instantly like and feel as though you have known for many lifetimes. She was already a published author, having self-published a series of craft instruction books inspired by the craft store in Greater Phoenix, which she owned.

In addition to being an accomplished author, she was a successful entrepreneur and created a highly successful residential and commercial painting company.

Doreene always had a smile and a hug waiting for anyone open to receiving her brilliant smile and open arms. Her parting words were always, *"Love ya!"*

As successful as she was in writing and running businesses, staying healthy and illness-free was not as easy for her. Throughout her lifetime, she overcame various health challenges. The worst of these came in 2003 when a cancer diagnosis knocked her to the ground. However, she was determined not to be just a survivor but a Victor!

Cancer took her on a new journey that would take many twists and turns. One of those turns would take her to Puerta Vallarta, Mexico, for alternative treatments. Those treatments would prove to be successful, if only for a few months.

I want to quote verbatim some of the journal writings she shared with over 10,000 subscribers in a column called, *"About Journaling."* She was open, honest, and vulnerable in sharing her Cancer Journey, as she referred to it. In a separate article entitled, "Victorious," she wrote Cancer Survivor and crossed out the word Survivor and replaced it with the word Victor. This article was published in other newsletters worldwide, sharing the beginning of her cancer journey.

Here are a few excerpts from that article and some of her cancer journal entries. Doreene asked that her writing not be edited because it is exactly as she wrote during this time. So, if you see an incorrect misspelled word or grammar, it is how she hand-wrote them at the moment. She always said that your journal entries are your private space, and you can write in any way that serves you.

Victorious!

"There it is again," I muttered to myself, frustrated as I washed my arm.

Every morning for five or six days, I noticed this rust-colored sticky stuff that appeared in both drips and smears on my left forearm and thigh. But I had no idea where it could be coming from. I considered the possibility that I'd gotten something on my clothes, the woodwork was seeping, or ...? I didn't have a clue. With each new day, I was just as surprised as the day before to find it again. As I tried to solve this growing mystery, my inability to discover the origin was frustrating. I was stumped.

Finally, on Sunday morning, I found the answer. My eyes followed my hand as I wiped the steam from the bathroom mirror. Looking past my fingertips, there it was. To my shock and horror, the rust-colored sticky stuff easily dripped from my left nipple.

In disbelief, I collapsed into my bedroom chair, swirling with a mix of grief and fear. I stared at the blank white wall, feeling vacant, distant, disconnected from what I had just seen in the mirror. All I heard was that loud, penetrating silence that surrounds and encompasses every thought and movement. Then, I began to wonder, what now? What's next?"

The above represents the first few paragraphs from her article, "Victorious." If you want a copy of the complete article, reach out to me, and I'll send it to you.

Below are a few of her cancer journal entries. Many of her entries were sent from Internet cafés in Puerta Vallarta, Mexico, where she received alternative cancer treatment. Writing these journal entries brought her much joy while going through the hideous hell of cancer. Writing was a welcomed distraction from the pain and allowed her to focus on sharing what she was experiencing in the hope that it would help others.

A Message from Doreene

These are my actual journal entries for two years: from August 2003, the time I found that something was wrong and I had cancer, till after I was cancer-free and a cancer victor, to August 2005, as I continued recovering from other childhood health challenges.

Please remember, Doreene asked that these entries not be edited for grammar, spelling, or punctuation as they are exactly as she originally wrote in her journal.

My Cancer Journey Journal
Today's Date 10.26.03

Here I am. I recently found out that I have cancer. After the initial shock, I set about figuring out what to do next to support me and this new health challenge. Right now I am in Mexico doing an alternative treatment that is already supplying results in unexpected ways. The process is demanding, but my attitude is great, as I will survive.

Below are a few of her daily entries:

8.24.03 – I keep finding this sticky, rust, colored stuff. Have no idea where it is coming from. Maybe I sat in something.

8.31.03 – I have drainage with blood coming out of my left breast. Dr. W is calling a cancer breast surgeon.

9.04.03 – Meet breast doc and she sent me to get a mammogram and ultra-sound, right then. (They did the tests over several times and I knew something was up as they were looking intently at both breast, I am still in shock)

9.18.03 – Doctor called and said I have breast cancer in my right breast, other problems in my left breast. I knew it.

Again, if you would like a copy of the entire journal series, please reach out to me, and I will send you one.

Due to the medical expense, by 2005, Doreene found herself without a home. At the time, I lived in a tiny mobile home and offered to share this space with her. We became the best roommates, and our friendship deepened.

In March 2007, cancer reared its hideous, ugly head and again became a part of Doreene's world. I had the honor and privilege to care for her. This part of her journey was difficult for us both.

Before she passed, she requested that I keep her legacy alive and take over publishing *The 5 Year Journal*. I'm proud to report that it is still available through any of your favorite booksellers. The original leatherette hardcover is no longer available; however, a new version with the original pages is available. Just Google "Doreene Clement" to find the latest version or contact me, and I can provide the best resource for you.

On June 14, 2007, Doreene flew into her next journey with Angel wings wrapped around her.

Doreene Clement
1951 - 2007

Sandy Rogers

Sandy is known as "The Referral Queen." She has served entrepreneurs in the holistic health, metaphysical, spiritual, personal development, and conscious business communities since 2000 through email promotions, consulting, and networking.

She is a birthmother who surrendered her only child to adoption in 1964. She advocates for adoption reform and, in 1985, helped create new law in Kentucky allowing adult adoptees to petition the courts for original birth certificates. In 2020, she testified in the Arizona Legislature for similar changes.

Sandy is a published author of *Love Meets Life, Wisdom of the Silver Sisters,* as well as this current edition of *The 5 Year Journal.*

Contact:
Sandy@AskSandyRogers.com
www.AskSandyRogers.com
www.The5YearJournal.com
www.Facebook.com/Sandy4Help

Scan the QR code with your smartphone or go to:
https://youtu.be/O3minOQxMIU

Divine Synchronicity

By Sharyn G. Jordan,
Storyteller

"We are the Write Person,
Forever, in the Write Place
Perennially, at the Write Time.
By Day: We are Alchemists
By Night: We are Visionaries
By Trade: We are Storytellers"

~ Sharyn G. Jordan

Chapter 30

ᴅivine Synchronicity

By Sharyn G. Jordan,

Storyteller

Driving through the undulating Texas Hill Country in the summer of 1961 was picture postcard perfect. Those magical days filled my twelve-year-old brave HeART with immense joy. As a dedicated *Dearest Diary-ist*, since 1953, I chronicled the entire adventure. There is something ever so indelible about journaling, writing, and scribing. As a form of divine alchemy, it forges the metal of not-so-excellent experiential into *Golden Wisdom,* allowing us to discover the *Silver-Lined* pockets of our blessings. This mystical quest included my cousin Jody, only thirteen-years-old, yet, worldly-wise. We were delighted to accompany her evangelical grandparents, the Rev. Emmett and Sister JoEllen, on their Miraculous Tent RE-vival Tour. It was divinely synchronistic.

Going down those enchanted, southern backroads with windows rolled down, tasting the honey-tipped gentle winds, and sipping iced cold lemonade fueled our Born-Again Spirits. In that blue grassed paradise, at the crystal-clear creek water's weave, magnificently, angels, butterflies, and hummingbirds winged their way round fields of glory. Nature's artistry bountifully bloomed fragrant wildflowers of pink Cosmos, Euphorbia's Baby Breath, and Mexican Sunflowers. Elegantly, they swayed in the woodland breezes; soared to the upbeat hymns playing on Austin's 101.1 Christian radio station. Anthems

261

of hope, musical messages of joy broadcast by the gospel singing Gaither Family's *Sweet Chariot* and *How Great Thou Art,* had Grandad's basso profundo, low, rich voice bringing these endearing songs to life.

My first and last *Bapticostal Spiritual Roadie* experience found me with a committed team, traveling in a ten-car and one semi-truck caravan, driving all over the Lone Star State to RE-connect precious Souls to Source. My parents doubted I would last *seven* days, yet for *seven* weeks and *seven* nights a week, I was in an apostolic RE-vival mode. Fascinated by these profoundly otherworldly portals, weekly, I wrote home describing my supernatural encounters. For over a hundred years, these old-fashioned tent forums, with their gypsy appeal, spoke to the unconventional person who perhaps found the traditional church too confining. The musical freedom of tambourines, guitars, and drums elicited toe-tapping joys, with our open hands held high in praise, and upon the Holy Ghost's visitation, we danced in Divine Love's wondrous worship. Systemically and miraculously, divine synchronicity was at play.

Those radiant RE-awakenings were tangible. If you have ever been *slain in the spirit,* you will know of its *ecstasy.* Although I always loved Jesus, was a prayer warrior, and considered miracles as real, witnessing those marvels firsthand, made a lasting ecclesiastical impression on me. To see the countenance of broken-hearted people anointed by Unconditional Love and BE Immediately converted to the Light was extraordinary. Seeing opulent omnipresence in the eyes of every soul who surrendered was transformational. It was not a religion; it was the Holy Spirit. I continue to speak in my prayer language called the *Gift of Tongues,* celebrate the timeless *Trinity of Yeshua, Mother, and Father God,* and of course, I still love my tambourine.

Oh, the times, they were ahhh' changing! *Seven* months after my mystery tour ended, my dear father, only thirty-eight years young, passed away. I was thirteen. The next *seven* years told a story of tumbling from an idyllic life into the abyss. Then, one year and *seven* months later, the entire world and I were devastated by President John Fitzgerald Kennedy's shocking assassination. The end of Camelot unearthed a grief I had never acknowledged, much less healed. It was a time of extremely dark nights of my soul. The RE-mainder of my teenage years was lived as a rebel with a cause. I railed against societal injustices, participated in Vietnam Pro-Peace rallies, marched for the Civil Rights movement, and deeply RE-sonated with Bob Dylan and Joan Baez's *Blowin' in the Wind.*

After a 1968 near-life-ending experience, detailed in the *Book of St. Suzanne, House of Forgiveness*, I sought professional help; over time, my mental, emotional, and spiritual health was RE-newed. I intensified my poetry, short story, and biographical writings. Since the alchemy of story is transformational, every aspect of those challenging years was RE-vealing. Generously, I was gifted enormous Grit, abiding Grace, and infinite Gratitude. A new chapter was about to unfold; divine synchronicity was preparing my HeART for a new life.

In 1969, a synchronistic series of events was unveiled. Years later, I learned they were orchestrated by our son Jason Nathaniel's *Celestial Parenting Agreement* declaring my late husband James 'Jay' Lewis Hathcock and me to be his Earth dad and mom. It was a promise dating back to the Golden Age of the Renaissance RE-corded in my historical fiction novel *Magda Rose, The Apothecary, Alchemist & Artist.* Suffice it to say, Jason's work was cut out for him. Thankfully, our miraculous meeting did come about in ways only Jason and the angels could have arranged. Jay and I RE-cognized one another as our Twin Flame; it was love at first sight! Since our heavenly love story is beautifully told in *The Book of Nathaniel, House of RE-demption*, I won't offer any spoilers.

Jay's and my first big decision as man and wife was to move to California. At a Hollywood party, we met Swami, a Tibetan monk en route to Mazatlán, Mexico, to teach a two-year I-Ching immersion course. By a continuously circuitous cycle of alchemical events, within one month, Jay and I were in Mazatlán, students of Swami. Divine Synchronicity was evident. During that transcendental time, my sweet born-again sister St. Suzanne and I began an illuminated correspondence. We explored the Cosmic connections between Biblical scripture and I-Ching Trigrams. *Psalms 16:11:* "In thy presence of fullness is joy." *I-Ching* #58: Joy "Know the Spirit of God is joyfully flowing through us in felicity, goodness, and laughter." These timeless teachings did not dispute one another; they expanded Truth into quantum fields of frequency. The exquisite energy I felt inexplicably moving through the RE-vival Tent was ever present in my Spirit. I BEcame a contemporary Christian Mystic.

After living in Mexico for two years, our precious sons Jason, age two, and Jeremy, a high-risk Preemie (in *St. Suzanne*'s poignant book), Jay and I RE-turned stateside. First to Texas, then in 1974, an unexpected overnight stay in Scottsdale, AZ, found me mesmerized by the BE-jeweled desert sky whose overhead canopy of brilliant stars was captivating. The intoxicating orange blossoms wafted wildly, my favorite song, the sumptuous *Midnight at The Oasis,* played; my Soul Beckoned to RE-locate into this Magical HeART-Scape. Indeed, it was divine synchronicity.

Blessed by another sweet son Ian Wells and darling daughter Olivia Suzanne; now many years later as our beautiful family's Matriarch, with fourteen GRANDchildren, and a Great-GRAND-Girl, our Legacy continues. Owning Rosebud Preschool, 5 Movie Theatres in northern Arizona, 11 years of RV traveling, and touring 48 States are real-life Faerie Tales. After 42 miraculous years, my Beloved Jay peacefully transitioned. Grateful BEyond Measure that Love Transcends the Veil! Dearest HeART, condensing life into 1,200 words is also a miracle. My Mission is to bring Heaven to Earth, Edify Humanity, BE a sacred Storyteller, an Alchemist, and a World Builder of a Pristine Future. Living in Divine Synchronicity is such an esteemed honor. ~Deep Bow.

Sharyn G. Jordan,
Storyteller

Not only is Sharyn an enthusiastic Story Alchemist, a Smith of the Word, but she also teaches others to discover their inner Muse.

Early on, she realized how the transformational process of intimately recording life's joys, sorrows, accomplishments, perceptions, fears, and tears revealed a much deeper understanding of life itself.

Known internationally as the Home Whisperer since 1994, she has merged practical magic, folklore, and scientific secrets in her Feng Shui Simplified Consultancy/ Her Wind-Water Conservatory Curriculum, WISDOM: the Way of the Writerly began in 2013. Having written historical fiction novels, a political thriller book, and biographies (nine altogether), she is deeply honored to create lasting legacies.

www.FengShuiSimplifed.com
Classroom@fengshuisimplifed.com

Scan the QR code with your smartphone or got to:
https://bit.ly/3NxBF1W

Cherished

By Sherri Ashton Smith

"A person places themselves on a level with the ones they praise."

~ Johann Wolfgang von Goethe

Chapter 31

Cherished

By Sherri Ashton Smith

Some people never know the lasting inspiration of a Legend's influence in their life. I am so fortunate to have had two.

The first person is my dad, Pressley Ashton, who was a brave pilot in World War II's Army Air Core. After the war, he delivered candy to Oklahoma and Texas farms and businesses. As fate would have it, my mother lived on one of the farms. She was stunning; daddy fell in love with her at first sight and asked her to marry him. To begin their new life chapter, they moved to a Company Town called Cactus, Texas, population of 3,000 families. Located at the top of the Texas Panhandle, only 60 miles from metropolitan Amarillo, it promised to be an adventure. Usually, company towns were built in areas with virtually no population, and entire communities housed their employees in the middle of nowhere. My dad's experience was in the chemical/oil industry, where the work was demanding and dangerous. Since times were hard and jobs were scarce, people came from all over.

My three younger, gorgeous sisters, Danyce, Candace, Kim, and I, had an idyllic childhood. Those precious memories still live in my heart today. Since Daddy was the company railroad engineer, we could sneak rides on his train. He was always an Officer of the local AFL/CIO elected to represent the Phillips 66 employees, where he fought for higher wages and better benefits but, mostly, for safer working conditions. When he traveled to Union Meetings, he took us to exciting and exotic places in his official position. Traditionally, company men flew, leaving their families at home. Every year, we took one or two trips to big cities for Union Conventions. Daddy loaded my mom, three sisters, and me up in whatever vehicle we had at the time, and off we went across the country only to arrive at well-known, luxurious hotels. Looking like Hillbillies with a couple of suitcases and a mountain of paper sacks with all our stuff, the valets were always astonished. Day and night, we ran through the hallways and rode up and down the elevators. We were quite the spectacle! We met and talked to famous politicians, including Lyndon Baines Johnson. Annually, our family's vacation was Yellowstone National Park. Other families traveled with us in a monstrous caravan from Texas to Montana. In the vast Big Sky Country, we pitched our tents and slept under a canopy of luminous stars. Time spent on Fishing Bridge, sightseeing, and bear and elk watching was magnificent.

After retirement, when company communities were being abandoned, Daddy and a small group of men formed the Cactus 287 Corporation. He even bought the town of Cactus. We had such fun telling new acquaintances our daddy was the mayor of the town that he owned. His entire life was devoted to fighting for better conditions for his family, his friends, and his community. Because of his love, leadership, and legacy, we were taught to be independent and grew up knowing we could do anything and be anyone. For the rest of his life and all through mine, my daddy was one of two of my biggest Legends.

My second Legend is my brilliant, creative, and talented Native American Assiniboine, Sioux husband, Charles Spotted Wolf.

Born on the Fort Peck Indian Reservation in Wolf Point, Montana, Charlie descends from a distinguished lineage, including his Great Grandfather, Col. David Dawson Mitchell, a famous Fur Trader who built Fort McKenzie in Montana and was an attendant negotiator at the 1851 Fort Laramie Treaty. With Lewis and Clark, he traveled up the Missouri to Yellowstone. His marriage to Rattling Bag (Marie Deschamp), daughter of the notorious Dechamp family, created quite the family tree.

At the 1904 St. Louis World's Fair, Charlie's maternal Grandmother, a member of the winning Fort Shaw World Champion Girls' Basketball Team, triumphed over boy teams from across the country. His uncle was a Hoover Dam Architect, and yet another uncle founded the Head Start Program in Wolf Point, Montana. His mother, Dorothy, grew up on the Reservation. She went on to work in Washington, DC, at the Bureau of Indian Affairs, where she met John David Smith, a tall, red-headed soldier on leave from the Army. After the war, JD got an excellent job with "Ma Bell" in Amarillo. To begin their new future, he moved his expanding family to the Caprock of Texas.

This is where young Spotted Wolf would grow up. As an asthmatic child, he missed many school days, yet his wise mother encouraged him to draw and paint. Over the years, his health improved, as did his love for the arts. Throughout his life, he has refined his God-given gifts, extending them into wood carving. His dedicatedly polished talent has won him many accolades.

Another natural skill set of Charlie's was sports; tall, handsome, and witty…rather shy too, I was intrigued with my fellow high school classmate. It was a mutual attraction; we soon became sweethearts and, thus, began our love story. When he received a full-ride football scholarship to the University of Utah, we had a fairy tale wedding, and off we went to Salt Lake City.

In 1970, we were blessed with a child, our amazing son, Dallas Charles, who was the love of our life. This beautiful boy gave us many years of happiness and love. He was not only a talented basketball and baseball star but an intelligent, humorous, handsome, and very kind human who sang solos in the church choir, was President of the Spanish Club, and went to college on a Basketball Scholarship.

Charlie's priority was taking care of our family, which limited his carving time. Therefore, in the early 1990s, he began designing our Christmas Cards. In that same timeline, we moved to Scottdale, Arizona, and invested in a southwest-style home on horse property, which was virtually our own company town because there was little development around us at the time. We proceeded to build a casita for my parents, Presley and LaVerne. It was the exact replica of our living room from the home we grew up in; the same avocado-colored couch and all! Daddy loved looking out the huge picture window at the desert wildlife that came to visit. Mother's exquisite prisms spanned the entire rod delighting when the sunlight sent rainbows dancing, casting their magic across this special room. Indeed, life was very good!

During a company-sponsored trip to the Sonoma Wine Country, our beautiful Dallas, only 25 years young, was tragically killed in a horrific boating accident. We both lost heart in almost everything except each other. We were simply crushed. After a few years, slowly, Charlie began to mend. Once again, he was drawn to paint and carve. Out of this recovery came his classic Totem Poles, admired by all who see them. His favorite place to select the special wood is a Phoenix lumber yard, which has an excellent selection. It must be a particular piece that holds the image speaking to his heart. He carves mainly from Pine or Redwood, some Ash, always creating such spectacular Totem Poles and masks.

We have been married for over 50 years. Even though our hearts have never fully healed from the loss of our spectacular son, we continue to adore and love each other.

Sherri Ashton Smith

My life has been an adventure with many twists and turns.

I have my Bachelor's Degree in Education and Business from West Texas State University and my Masters's from California State University.

I spent the first part of my career teaching Business Classes in High School and then college.

The second part of my career was working with a world-famous Golf Course Resort Design and Construction Company as the Assistant to the Presidents. I traveled to many famous golf courses and met most of the famous golfers.

Born in 1948, I spent the first part of my life as my Daddy' Girl. The second part of my life has been spent as Spotted Wolf's Girl.

Spotted Wolf and I have now retired to Scottsdale, Arizona, to a fun and exciting life. He continues with his art to make me cherished, happy, and safe.

Website: www.charlesspottedwolf.com
Email: charles@charlesspottedwolf.com

Double Talk

By Suzanne Anderson

*"Embrace who you are above everything
because that is what you are — Everything."*

~ Suzanne Anderson

Chapter 32

Double Talk

By Suzanne Anderson

We already know the story. It was told to us long, long ago, yet there was a longing, a yearning to experience it for ourselves. We wanted to act it out physically by being part of the story. Like a comet, we entered the lower realms. Like a comet, we're given a name, and we sparkle brightly in glory and majesty until we're gone. Where do comets come from, and where do they go?

The Greco-Roman God of portals was Janus. He is depicted as having a head with two faces, one looking East and the other West. His temple had two main gates, one at either end and was open to the sky. During the time of war, both gates were open, and when they were closed, it was a time of peace. Janus had his bright side and his dark side. In the spring of the year, he presided over carnage and conquest, and in the fall it was a time of peace and plenty. He was known as the God of beginnings and endings.

In ancient engravings or statuary Janus is shown holding a power symbol shaped like a key in one hand or a rod with a doorknob on top. Each footrests on a sphere that looks like a world, so he is poised between the two. In worship services, he was invoked before any of the other gods and was considered a primordial deity.

My dad was the God of my world. It was in Chicago during the depression that the Automatic Canteen company was founded. His idea of coin-operated vending machines that served chocolate candy to factory workers would be a good business.

> *"Who could make the sunrise, sparkle it with dew,*
> *Cover it with chocolate and a miracle or two?*
> *The candy man can. He makes the world feel good!"*

During the dark years of the great depression, between 1929 and 1939, my dad, Franklin Howard Anderson, was busy building an empire. He made business arrangements with Hershey, Mars, Peter and Paul, Holloway, and Wrigley to supply their confections for the vending machine outlets. Many new candy corporations were being formed and listed on the Stock Exchange. Extreme hardship birthed extreme prosperity for some of us, and we were singing "HAPPY days are here again" by the time I was 10 years old. Even my idol, the legendary Shirley Temple, sang, "On the good ship lollipop, take a nice trip to the candy shop!" Strangely, lollipops were also associated with scary things like the dentist's office.

Then in the 40s came the start of another conflict. We were afraid of getting bombed by the Japs. Hershey's chocolate in a hard shell was introduced during the war as rations for the troops. Bruce Murrie, son of the President of Hershey corporation, got together with Forrest Mars to market M&M candies to the general public. My dad was more significant than the general public and an Executive Director, so our family had M&Ms first!

At Christmas, Dad ordered from Hershey's gifts of giant Golden wrapped chocolate almond bars almost the size of a pizza box. We were gifted a caramel Holloway sucker so big that we kids used a hammer and chisel to chop off edible chunks.

Such treasures were hidden away in the storeroom along with tins of Beich hard candy pillows which were reserved for special occasions like Christmas.

"Candy isn't good for you," dad would say, and I was restricted from getting into the storeroom and would be punished if I did. How could such a yum-yum be a no-no at the same time?

Dad made the rules, and he was above the rules. For example, smoking and drinking were bad for people, but he did it all the time. He could swear a lot. When I used a swear word, I was rebuked. "Do as I say, not as I do."

One of his directives was that I would have to learn how to swim. It was an essential survival skill in his mind. We lived near Lake Michigan and had a summer cabin on Mirror Lake in Wisconsin. Boating was a summer pastime. Water was fearsome. I couldn't breathe under the water, so I knew I would surely die without breathing. There were times when I was little; I would have a crying fit that wouldn't stop until my dad picked me up and dunked my head into a bathroom sink full of water. That is how I learned to "stifle." Self-control came about just by the threat of the water treatment and that look from dad.

One time we were canoeing on mirror lake in Wisconsin, and dad had an idea he could teach me to swim by tying a rope around my waist and putting me over the side.

"Just paddle your arms and kick your feet and you can swim," he said. I was terrified, and I was afraid he would let go of the rope, and I would sink. Of course, I was right, for as soon as I paddled away from the side of the boat, there was no more tug on the rope. I was doing it all by myself until I thought my daddy would not keep me safe. Under I went, and I didn't learn how to swim until I was 12 years old and had a different teacher at the Wilmette Country club swimming pool. Now I love the water, and I can become one with it because now I know I am actually physically made of it.

Oneness in duality is explained by quantum physics when they say matter is light and light is both particle and wave at the same time. Yes, it all depends upon perspective.

Like the comet, my dad left this life when I was 15 years old. I recognize his brilliance, and today I am supported by the Anderson family trust, safe and secure financially. I learned to embrace what he taught me. I discovered the enduring truth that working with the positive aspect of a thing while still embracing the negative aspect lets us stay in balance.

That is why the key energy of the portal or gateway is represented by Janus, the dual-face God of beginnings and endings.

Some may ask, where is the love in this story? Perhaps it's in the Hershey kisses, the discipline, the family enjoying boating, the water itself, the breath of life, and the worship of God. I would say yes to all of the above. Love is everywhere when you look between the lines!

Suzanne Anderson

Suzanne Anderson is 94 years young, who says she is now getting younger.

Always an educator, she was Certified in three levels in Montessori Education - hands-on methods for Preschool, Kindergarten, and Elementary Education. She was the director of her school in Bozeman, MT. She won an award for writing curriculum with American Montessori for her master's project on the Mineral Kingdom.

Her first love is Sacred Geometry, and she studied with the acclaimed British Master Teacher Keith Critchlow at the KAIROS Foundation.

She is writing a new book titled *Connecting the Dots - Manifesting Destiny with Sacred Geometry*. Suzanne is a perpetual student who is constantly learning and teaching. She is working on a video project with her daughter called "Self-Sovereignty Series" Coursework.

Direct inquires to her daughter Lindsay@Lindsaygodfree.com

https://lindsaygodfree.com/event/manifesting-with-sacred-geometry-sound-vibration-and-light-frequency/

Scan the QR code with your smartphone or go to:
https://youtu.be/0R_UDcM81Co

Back to the Start

By Travis Sutton

"I am still far from being what I want to be,
but with God's help I shall succeed."

~ Vincent Van Gogh

Back to the Start

By Travis Sutton

A blonde-haired kid dreams of the endless possibilities that stream inside of a small box containing a screen, a few toggle switches, and a cartridge holder. The year was 1993. At four years old, I had just received my first of many gaming systems, the Nintendo Gameboy. For me, this was the beginning of a long yet circular relationship with modern technology. It was the beginning of my journey to mesh the seemingly opposing forces of creativity with analytics and detail. It was the beginning of what makes me…well, me.

So many times, we see technology as an impersonal object that operates in the black and white, a zeros and ones' sphere of an unfeeling machine. However, in some of the best and worst scenes of my early upbringing, I found a growing refuge in the digital world. Just one year after receiving that first Gameboy, I was one of the last people to see my grandfather, Lehman Sutton, alive. His passing wrecked me emotionally. I couldn't quite grasp the explained concept of death of the man who made up my life's first memory. All I had was a surreal level of sadness. A channeling outlet for the overbearing and unprocessed feelings for the next few years became my new friend: the Gameboy.

By the time I was ten, our family was plagued by just short of what I would call a curse. 1999 was supposed to be an epic year for the ages that turned into a flurry of challenges. It was anticipated to be my dad's most profitable and abundant year as a farmer in rural Eastern North Carolina. Life was great. It felt as if we were on top of the world and headed into outer space, until we weren't. Profitability wasn't in God's plan. Instead, a five-hundred-year flood called Hurricane Floyd was. Thankfully, so was my saint-of-a-mother, Marjorie, who picked up a second and third job just so that we could survive. Chaos was all around. Money had seemingly dried up. Still, the constant was my ability to escape through a digital portal in my room; one that allowed me to explore the known world and have hope without spending a dime.

This portal wasn't only about drowning sorrow, it was also a catalyst to memories which still put a smile on my face to this day. Way before the days of streaming, me and my brother, Joe, would stay up until the orange glow of the sun peeked through the blinds, downloading music on a dial up connection. There was one night, I will never forget. We were trying to find the right version of a specific song. Every time we downloaded it, the song would glitch. We troubleshot; 4am, 5am, 6am, we finally got it. There were hours of loading time that night, but that meant there were hours upon hours of getting to bond with my brother, my best friend and someone who was a needed example for me during a critical time in my life. I wouldn't trade that for the world; hell, I wouldn't trade that for the universe.

Joe helped me uncover so many things about myself that may lay dormant forever. He was and is a model for me. If he drew a deer, I drew a deer. If he got a drafting table, I wanted a drafting table. Nine years my senior, he was always a better artist; however, his talent gave me the drive to better myself and stimulated my curiosity to explore my skills beyond being entertained by the magical electric box.

Throughout high school I continued to explore the seemingly opposed forces of technology and creativity. Drawing and writing, specifically, was something I thoroughly enjoyed. These were tools that allowed an additional escape and a way of creating a world that felt more like my own, one where I was certainly more in control. I would draw on my arms and cover it with a hoodie like I had tattoos. I would write poems for topics that were extremely important, like the baseball team or my "super serious" dating life, joking here. The kicker though: I never revealed any of my work or even talked about my creative side with others, not even those closest.

Today, I flashback to the many points in time that my dad, Richard, told me to become an accountant, an attorney, or a medical doctor. No, there's no blame game. My dad wanted a better life for me, one that didn't involve the hardships of farming. These careers represented those paths to him. It left me with two degrees from top programs in the country in accounting, and I love him to death for continuing to push me. As you could imagine, there is a "but" here. I believe I was trying to fit a mold that wasn't exactly what I needed to be for myself.

Three years after I took my first accounting job, I found myself in thought, alone, in a dimly lit hotel room in Prescott, Arizona. I told my fiancé, Chelsea, that I need to take some time to myself. Looking back, I probably could have phrased that a little better. It scared the ever living you-know-what-out of her, but I needed to get clear on who I was. Right there, I decided I needed something "new" even if I didn't know what that "new" was.

After relinquishing my position, what I had hoped for, but didn't realize I needed, found me. My two opposing talents finally reached their crash course destination in the form of designing digital experiences. Thank God, because my bank account had a minus in front of it. Thank God, because that was the impetus for the thought, "let's push my tech knowledge forward as well and learn how to code."

The switch gave me my superpowers back. It allowed me to create my own worlds once again. It also allowed me to satiate my detail and analytical needs. The transition into a new career, that wasn't on my radar, was the combination that I had been missing for so long.

The beauty for me wasn't necessarily in the journey. The beauty was understanding what the journey was trying to teach me. My career transition taught me:

1. Never be ashamed of yourself, your family or where you were born.
2. Just because you're good at something, doesn't mean you're not good at something else that can bring more fulfillment.
3. It's okay to take time for you to do some soul searching every now and then, and I pray that you will.

This chapter is dedicated to my grandparents, S.A. Paramore Jr., and Carrie Dail Paramore.

Travis Sutton

Travis Sutton is an author, husband to Chelsea Sutton, and self-taught digital creative in ConsultMent, based out of Phoenix, Arizona.

Born and raised in Farmville, North Carolina, Travis holds an accounting degree from Top 20 – WP Carey School of Business at Arizona State, and a master's degree in taxation from Top 15 – Sturm College of Law at University of Denver. In his spare time, he loves reconnecting with nature on hikes around Phoenix and riding horses.

Website: travsutton.com
LinkedIn: linkedin.com/in/travsutton
Twitter: twitter.com/travsutton

Scan the QR code with your smartphone or go to:
https://youtu.be/vl8MTBix1Gw

Legends of Lemuria and Atlantis

Root Races

By Viviane Chauvet

"Radiate boundless love towards the entire world."

~ Gautam Buddha

Chapter 34

Legends of Lemuria and Atlantis

Root Races

By Viviane Chauvet

Lemuria and Atlantis's glorious legends and stories remind humanity of an elevated era of divine consciousness on Earth. Many people worldwide still feel the influences of those advanced civilizations in their hearts and soul. Now that the Earth has completed a twenty-six-thousand-year evolutionary cycle, as the Mayans predicted, humans have once again entered a new era of awakening.

3D Earth humans have begun their spiritual ascension process as a species to reclaim their original blueprint and 12 DNA consciousness. In the time of Lemuria, life co-existed in harmony with all beings who were in complete connection with the sacred pulse of Earth/Mother Gaia. The Lemurians were depicted as highly advanced beings, peaceful, and very spiritual. They became prolific at using the power of heart energy and crystals as archives for encoded information. The continent of Lemuria, also known as Mu (Motherland), apparently existed before and during the time of Atlantis. According to many researchers, Mu would have existed between North America and Asia (or Australia) in the Southern Pacific. Some researchers believe that the original continent might have been closer to Japan.

In today's myths, many still believe that the Lemurian knowledge exists as seed crystals within the Earth's core. Until humanity reaches a higher peek of spiritual maturity and emotional stability, those legendary crystals remain hidden in the higher dimensional space of the power grids of this planet. As a root race to humanity, the Lemurians were associated with DNA strand 2. History has shown that the Aborigines in Australia also preserved their sacred knowledge similarly to the Lemurians, meaning underground and in holy crystals.

While Lemuria (Mu) and Atlantis had existed at the same time in Earth's history, the Lemurians had apparently chosen Atlantis as the selected colony for the creation and genesis of a brand-new civilization. Both societies abide by the consciousness of One without boundaries or limitations, harmony, wisdom, higher consciousness, and unconditional love in their golden eras. The Lemurians had chosen to live in connection with the power of their Heart centers, and the Atlanteans chose the Mind path. They also used crystals as a source of energy and storage for ancient knowledge. The Atlanteans co-existed in harmony alongside other advanced beings such as the Galactic Mer (mermaid), dolphins, aquatic beings, and so forth. In its original conception, Atlantis was meant to be the first colony to host the Mystery Schools, a precursor to the Mystery Schools of Egypt. Historically, the Atlanteans were perceived as moral and spiritual people of great wisdom and the root race for DNA strand 3. Both strands 2 and 3 correspond to the incarnate identity (physical, emotional, and mental bodies).

Legends say that the Atlanteans misused their highly advanced mental faculties. They wanted to gain more power without the great wisdom of their hearts. The High Priests and High Priestesses foresaw that Atlantis would fall to Ego – a fragmented Mind that believes it is separated from Source. The distorted pattern created waves of disharmonic energies that cast the Earth into the third density. Many authors and researchers believe that the legendary island was in the Atlantic Ocean, and its core region was in South-West Morocco.

Other common theories suggest that Atlantis was the Greek island of Santorini, while the "real" continent was off the Bahamas. Of course, Atlantis was known for its incredible beauty and crystalline temples. Many galactic groups partnered with the Atlanteans to manifest paradise on Earth and unity consciousness. What can we learn and apply the most from their past lessons? We need to live, co-create, choose, speak and act upon the wisdom of the heart combined with the higher faculties of the Mind. It is imperative to transcend lower egoic and primal instincts that create reactive and, sometimes, impulsive decisions.

Today, Lemuria and Atlantis' ancient legacies and sacred knowledge still resonate in the minds and hearts of many souls, including within the Quantum DNA Field and cellular memory. With all the global and planetary changes, the actual 3D human body is vibrational shifting to a new cosmic human template. The goal is to heal any distortions in the body blueprint and finally reach physical ascension out of the 3D realm. We reintegrate all soul fragments for conscious unification and divine wholeness by healing emotional trauma and ancient historical layers. As an ascended master, Buddha taught that wisdom, kindness, patience, generosity, and compassion were essential virtues for enlightenment. All of us are invited to return to living by those important virtues and sacred Cosmic Laws. Many people are rediscovering their true nature as Divine Essence of Light experiencing a human life. My goal is to inspire everyone to see and accept the infinite potential embedded in the core of their beings and assist people in accessing this inner reservoir of energy and gifts.

Sacred knowledge, Divine Grace, and ancient teachings remind us that it is all about raising our consciousness. We, of the ancient interstellar communities, hold humanity, Gaia, and all evolving sentient life forms in the highest light of the Golden Ray of Divine Wisdom and Love.

Viviane Chauvet

Viviane Chauvet is internationally recognized for her ascension work as an advanced Arcturian hybrid avatar, multidimensional healer, speaker, and published author.

CEO of Infinite Healing from the Stars LLC, she is the founder of the Arcturian Energy Matrix Healing® technique and host of The Infinite Star Connections Podcast.

Visit: InfiniteHealingFromtheStars.com
YouTube Channel:
www.youtube.com/c/VivianeChauvetGalacticHealer
Facebook: www.facebook.com/vivianechauvetgalactichealer
Instagram: www.instagram.com/viviane_chauvet

Scan the QR code with your smartphone or go to:
https://youtu.be/FYmlpEjIH-k

Homage Authors

That's what we Storytellers do. We restore order with imagination. We instill hope again and again and again. "

~ Walt Disney

The Dreamcatcher Codes

By Barbara Newman

Something happens when you listen to your wild soul. It whispers with an urgency; the flame gets fanned, and the fire transforms.

I didn't know that writing The Dreamcatcher Codes would change me. But it did. The vision came to me in a lucid dream: four courageous girls coming together from the four directions, powered by earth, air, fire, and water, on a search for the stolen Codes of Nature that would restore the natural world.

How could I write about Mother Earth if I didn't know her intimately, if I didn't feel her breath in my bones?

I went out of my comfort zone...and found my peace.

I slept under the stars in the high desert without a tent and tasted the Milky Way for the first time. It dripped like caramel off my tongue. My senses were bathed in moonlight and mystery, woodsmoke, and coyote calling to the night.

I took hikes in remote places—and in the solitude, the messages came. The winds, water, and stones all had a story. And something to teach.

My nature as a woman rose. I learned that we are not separate, plant, animal, human, or earth; we are all in relationship.

I began to notice the sacred geometry of a zinnia, the thirteen 'moons' on a turtle's shell, and how nature was the architect of the world.

As I took my characters on a daring journey into a deeper understanding of their own unique place in the universe, I discovered my own place; and woke up my wild soul.

Barbara Newman

Barbara Newman spent years as a Creative Director, building iconic global brands. When she heard an interview on NPR about the American cowgirl, she was so inspired she left the ad world for Montana and began filming a documentary about their lives.

It was out West where she fell in love with the natural world, the power of the landscape, and what it means to be an environmental steward. It was also where she connected with indigenous elders and their teachings.

Barbara is an advocate for building cultural bridges and empowering women and girls and was part of the think tank that developed the Fred Rogers Center for Children's Media and Education. She lives in the Berkshire Mountains of Western, MA, on Stockbridge-Munsee Mohican land. Her award-winning book, The Dreamcatcher Codes, is her love letter to mother earth and all her daughters.

www.BarbaraNewmanAuthor.com

Doorways to Daily Soul Nurturance

Perpetual Calendar

By Cristina Whitehawk

"There comes a time for replenishment
replenishment for our *soul*
replenishment for our *heart*
replenishment for our *life.*"

~ Cristina Whitehawk

Embedded within *Doorways to Daily Soul Nurturance* is a process of great growth. Perhaps initially, you will find the learning so subtle, it appears, in hindsight, to have been below your awareness level. At other times, the learning may appear to be difficult and almost impossible. This can be part of the growth process necessary to be one with the Divine Timing of the Creator-God within.

"Please listen closely to your heart; it will gently guide you. Doubt not your own divine timing (no matter what it looks like to the outside world). Hold fast to your dreams, especially those which seem like they will "never" come to be. Dream them awake and step out in faith.

Praise from readers I love this calendar! I go through it one day at a time, year after year, and it still inspires me. " ~ Julie Newendorp, Santa Barbara, CA

"I'm enjoying Doorways SO much. It's like opening a gift every day when I turn the page to begin my day."
~ Barbara Smith, LAc. Victor, ID

Cristina Whitehawk

Cristina Whitehawk, a two-time award-winning author, joyfully shares 40+ years of wisdom through her books, workshops, and speaking. She loves facilitating others in their soul growth to discover new rich ways of being in the world.

Contact: Cristina@PoweredByGenius.com
Website: www.PoweredByGenius.com
Facebook: www.facebook.com/cristina.whitehawk

Jody Sharpe

Years ago, writing became healing after the loss of my precious daughter, Kate. I'd written little stories as a child and poems as an adult, but the tragic loss of Kate set me on a different path. As I walked the grieving path, determined not to become a bitter old woman, the synchronicity of events would change my life.

Because of a voice in a dream from an angel, I read a book that gave me inspiration. And with love from family and kindness from friends and strangers, I found my way. At first, I thought I would write about grief, but miraculously, I met a man one day whose comforting words turned my face toward heaven. I am sure now Kate sent me an angel.

With the angel encounter in mind, I decided to write novels about angels. My Mystic Bay Series starting with 'The Angel's Daughter,' centers around angels who live as humans in a town where no one knows the secret. Then my sister encouraged me to write a memoir of my life-changing teaching career called, 'Special Needs Children the Angels on My Shoulder.' Next, I wrote a children's book, 'When the Angel Sent Butterflies.'

All of the writers in this book have compelling stories to tell us. Each burst of wisdom came from each author's own joys, hardships, and, thus, enlightenment. Writing changed my life for the better. I know in my heart Kate is here as I write each word, my angel on my shoulder.

Jody Sharpe

Writing about angels became healing after losing her daughter and then her husband. The valuable lessons Jody learned about moving forward, and loving life in the now have set her on a mission to tell stories with love, humor, and spiritual awakening.

Jody hopes to enlighten readers to contemplate the precious life and memories we are given.

Jody Sharpe is an awarding-winning author whose books include:

Special Needs Children the Angels on My Shoulder, the Mystic Bay Series, The Angel's Daughter, To Catch an Angel, Town of Angels, Town of Angels Christmas, and *20 Moon Road an Angel's Tale.* Her children's book is *When the Angel Sent Butterflies.*

www.JodySharpe.com

Judith Manganiello

"This is my life's journey back to myself.
I realized midway I was never alone in this journey.
I had my inner partner helping me all along the way."

~Judith Manganiello

Are You Ready to Love Yourself?

After selling my store, A Peace of the Universe, I was inspired by a loving and compassionate message I received from Spirit, "Judith, the givers are not getting the wisdom on how to receive Self-Love, and you must teach them."

I realized it was time to share my stories in a book on how I was able to learn all my lessons in receiving love for myself. The special ones were great at giving love to me but still needed to learn how to receive love for themselves.

Here are some questions to see if this book will help you on your journey.

- Are you a giver?
- Do you only know how to give?
- Does your heart only know how to serve others?
- Do you have trouble saying no to someone?
- Are you a peacemaker?

- Do you make peace at the expense of yourself?
- Do you sacrifice yourself for others?
- Do you know that it is important that you learn to love yourself but have no idea how to do it?

If you answered yes to any questions, this book will help you on your journey back to loving yourself.

I could not have written my book or shared my stories if it was not for the help of all the givers that were Divinely guided into my life. Bless you and thank you to all the givers for giving me all your love.

I am happy to say I am finally open to receiving it.

Judith Manganiello

Judith Manganiello, a New Jersey native, is an author, Reiki Master, Open Channel, Intuitive, Numerologist, and Ordained Minister.

In 1992 Judith acquired a spiritual and metaphysical bookstore in Scottsdale, Arizona, called A Peace of the Universe (APOTU), a Center for Spiritual Growth where she hosted various speakers for workshops and book signings.

In her first book, "A Giver's Way Home: Journey for Self-Love," she shares her journey to discovering self-love and how that changed her life and her purpose.

Judith's Real Love of Self class takes participants on a journey to discover their self-love and how to know and trust their divinity, discover their purpose, and find their Light.

Website: www.JudithAndSpirit.com
Email: Judith999apotu@gmail.com
Phone: 480-338-9815

Epilogue

From its origin, the Guiding Grace Series' intention continues to inspire, support, and walk alongside each of our global Writerly's. We celebrate our authors for embarking upon what Joseph Campbell refers to as "The Hero's Journey." Indeed, answering Destiny's Call creates larger, deeper, and more meaningful experiences. Thank you for BEing a Fellow Sojourner.

Holding sacred space for our Storytellers who have embraced, expressed, and expanded their voices is an esteemed honor.

Written generously, courageously, and vulnerably from their luminous life, these chapters will readily light up your Readerly Way.

Our Goldens' keen expertise, unique experientials, and impactful engagements elevates insightfulness, elongates mindfulness, and enriches life itself. As you Scribe Your Golden Wisdom Story, we invite you to also BE as follows:

Love:

RE•sonate with this transformational beauty as seeing others through the lens of love is alchemical. Let us sow blessings into the fertile soil of abundance.

Legends:

RE•joice in Life's Sorrows and Joys. BE•stow brave•HeARTedness, instill bold Grace, and seed tender Mercy.

Legacy:

REceive and BE•Queath an inheritance of Valour, Value, & Vision. These virtues blossom empathy and will positively change the world.

In Grace & Gratitude,
Sandy Rogers
Sharyn G. Jordan
Triangulus 3 Publishing, LLC

Special Acknowledgements

We are deeply honored to sing the praises of our Golden Wisdom publisher, the beautiful Becky Bee (yes, this is her fabulous middle name) Norwood. She is productively active, never just a busy bee!

In our first Guiding Grace Series volume, Wisdom of the Silver Sisters, we were ecstatic to write (and it still holds true), "In a virtual space where publishing platforms promise to deliver our book babies to a waiting world, it is worthwhile to know Becky Bee's wunderkind system works in Real Time!"

From start to finish, her exquiste expertise gracefully guided us. Becky is a No. #1 International Bestselling author, speaker & book publishing expert; and CEO of Spotlight Publishing House™. Having brought 400 authors to #1 Best•Seller status, she BElieves that a well•told story is a gateway for growth, a way to unite humanity & advocate positivity.

There are simply not enough words to describe how grateful we are for the RE•markable Becky. As our Triangulus 3 Publishing, LLC Agent, working with her is forever divine. Becky's trustworthiness, professionalism, and in-depth understanding of an ever•evolving industry is profound.

For those of you desiring to publish your Golden Wisdom memoir and/or a biography of Love, Legend, & Legacy, we whole•heartedly, emphatically and confidently recommend Becky. Her brilliant system is even lauded by other esteemed publishers! Indeed, by the book, she continues to "BEE the Change We Want to See in the World!" ~ Gandhi

If you wish to reach out to Becky this is how you can connect:
becky@spotlightpublishinghouse.com
https://SpotlightPublishingHouse.com

Deep Bow,
Sandy & Sharyn

~Write Onward. 🖋

Made in the USA
Middletown, DE
12 November 2022

14787471R00176